INDISPENSABLE

The prescription for a fulfilling
pharmacy career

Alex Barker, PharmD

DEDICATION

To Megan, she won't read this whole book, but she's the whole reason why I wrote it.

DOWNLOAD THE FREE TOOLS...

The book in your hands is my best effort to help you to finally take control of your career, of your life, and to become indispensable! As you will read I have committed my life to help pharmacist like you to take control of yours.

Below I have put together a collection of an *Indispensable* guide and additional tools you can download for free as a reader of this book.

These free tools reinforce and make actionable the ideas you will find in the pages of this book.

They have been indispensable in my journey, and I know they can help you too.

Download your free tools here:
www.indispensablepharmacist.com

I wish you success on your journey.

Warm caffeinated regards,

Alex Barker, PharmD

CONTENTS

About This Book 9

Preface 11

Introduction 13

How to Use This Book 19

I'm a Terrible Pharmacist 21

PART ONE - David, Meet Goliath 27

    Are You Burned Out? 31

    What Are the Results of a Burned-out Lifestyle? 37

    What Can You Do About It? 41

    S-T-U-C-K 43

    Sit Down and Shut Up 49

    Fear, Loathing, and Micromanagement 53

    Health Care? Try "Number Care" 57

    It's Time to Take Charge 63

PART TWO - Find Your Path 65

    Curiosity, Play, and Joy 69

    Your Unique Ability and Zone of Genius 83

Your Ikigai 91

One Life 107

A Powerful New Way of Living 113

PART THREE - Clear Your Way 121

What Are You Afraid Of? 125

Finances and Failure: Tackling Your Practical Fears . 135

Overcome Weaknesses, Failures, and Rejections 143

Develop "New" Strengths 153

Uncover Your Best Habits 163

PART FOUR - Become Indispensable 165

Meet New People 173

Take Care of Your Reputation 183

Create Value 191

Go Beyond the Manager 207

Become an Expert 209

No One Will Give Me a Chance 213

Should I Start a Business? 217

Conclusion 221

Prologue 227

Biography 229

ABOUT THIS BOOK

This book is for the pharmacist who feels like the profession has rejected them. It is for the pharmacist who…

- Feels like she can't handle another day of work.

- Can't imagine working in pharmacy for another twenty years.Feels trapped in her job.

- Fears he made a mistake choosing the pharmacy profession.

- Never wants to look at another prescription again.

- Worries there are no career options in pharmacy for him.

- Wants to know what she can do to change her situation.

- Desires fulfilling work and is dedicated to finding it (or creating it).

This book is for any pharmacist willing to do the work to identify what he or she wants and then take action to get it. We're in this together.

PREFACE

By reading this book, you will learn how to create an *indispensable* pharmacy career.

The indispensable pharmacist is someone who...

- Feels happy at the end of the workday.

- Receives regular job opportunities from a growing network.

- Must say "no" to project and job opportunities because she receives too many.

- Constantly wonders about her passion and work, thinking, "What will tomorrow hold?"

- Can't wait to apply new knowledge at work.

- Doesn't let a manager's rejection stop her from trying something else.

- Feels at sync with her work, her team, her manager, and most importantly her patients (or clients).

- Feels like he's making the greatest impact in the world because he's doing what makes him amazing.

I'm going to teach you how to create an indispensable career.

If you feel like this isn't possible, trust me, I understand because I was a dispensable pharmacist.

Now I consider my career *indispensable* because my full-time work at The Happy PharmD causes me to feel alive. I help pharmacists create inspiring careers. I've helped pharmacists who would call themselves unremarkable, who had next to nothing when it comes to career development, move into new, fulfilling careers, some without prior experience. Now they love what they do.

This book is your career guide, showing you the core strategies to create an indispensable career. Yes, you'll need to update your resume and LinkedIn, but those things don't make you indispensable. Before we jump into what *will* make you indispensable, I will share how I went from hating my work and life to loving work in pharmacy again.

INTRODUCTION

When I began writing this book, I thought it would be called *Indispensable: How to create a fulfilling pharmacy career in a saturated market.* I'd share the strategies and tactics my pharmacist clients have used to set themselves apart from the pack and rise up the ranks of their chosen path. Easy-peasy.

But I had a nagging feeling in the first two weeks of writing. I got about 16,000 words down before I hit my first "writer's block." My mind started swirling with thoughts like, "This book won't help anyone... No one will read this... You can't write a good book about pharmacy careers," and my creativity came to a full stop. Funny how hard it can be to write a book once you convince yourself that no one will want to read it.

I was determined to get it done, though, so I hired a coach to help me. After only one or two sessions, he asked me to do something I didn't expect: "Alex," he said, "You need to write about what scares you about this book." I listened to him and wrote down my fears. There were a lot of them, but the one big statement that came out of this writing session was this:

Your career isn't admirable enough to value. No one looks up to your pharmacist career and thinks, "Wow, I hope I can be like him someday."

That terrified me. Even scarier was that it was true. My "traditional" pharmacist career isn't admirable.

After residency, I was hired as a clinical pharmacy specialist at a rural medical center. I was placed in ambulatory care, but I didn't stay there long. I received no on-the-job training for four to five months and sat alone in an empty office searching for things to do. My "mentor" didn't train me or like me, and later dissuaded my manager from keeping me in primary care. So I was shipped off to an anticoagulation clinic instead, far away from my mentor. I wasn't against the move, since I did little of significance at the time. Everything else just seemed to fall into place around me, keeping me where I was.

Academia had always been my "end game" career path. I love teaching, speaking, and mentoring. I feel alive when I stand in front of a class, as though my soul catches fire and everything in the world seems right. But while I knew I'd found my calling, I had a problem with pursuing academia right after residency. Namely, I lacked real-world experience worth passing on to the next generation of pharmacists. I hated the idea of becoming a professor right after graduation—what value would I bring to the profession? I also knew I wouldn't be happy in an academic institution. I believe the education system is seriously flawed and ripe for innovative disruption. I didn't think I could or wanted to be the solution.

And so I felt trapped on this pharmacy career path. I couldn't move, and I couldn't find a pharmacy job that sounded better than what I had—at least, not one that was within two hours of my house. For the first three years of my post-residency profession, I resented my career choices. I'd beat myself up as I walked into my work building: "Alex, you brought this on yourself. You picked this as your career."

My morning commutes were filled with time-travel fantasies. I would go back to my younger self and say, "WAKE UP! The pharmacy future you've chosen is not what you pictured. Pick something else. You will not enjoy this kind of work." I'd listen to TED talks from professionals excited about their careers and work, and wonder, "Why don't I have that kind of passion for my job? What's stopping me from changing the world around me? Why can't I be amazing at what I do?" Then I'd shut off the computer and go back to my regular routine.

No matter how much I daydreamed and fantasized, my present didn't change. I was stuck.

Until... I decided to change.

Instead of spending my morning commute daydreaming, I started listening to self-development and entrepreneurial podcasts like Freakonomics, NPR, Dave Ramsey, 48 Days with Dan Miller, and Smart Passive Income with Pat Flynn. I learned how "normal" people started blogs and created income for themselves. The countless stories of people all over the world who were "over" the corporate setting and created a business for themselves were so uplifting and exciting. I felt inspired by what they had achieved for themselves and immediately fell in love with the idea of doing it, too. I thought, "Maybe I could create my own university." So I set to work.

I focused on learning everything I could about entrepreneurship. There was so much that appealed to me—but I loved the idea of working for myself most. Since I felt trapped in my career, what better way for me to progress than by carving my own way out? I could work in my own business, built *my* way, rather than working in a corporate or academic setting where I'd be forced to adhere to someone else's rules.

Most of all, I loved the idea that my actions could result in direct outcomes. This gave me a real sense of purpose. The more I worked, the more money I earned, and, unlike my anticoag job, where I could be the worst pharmacist on the team and earn as much as the best pharmacist, this new pursuit would require me to be my best.

Slowly but surely, I created businesses that fueled my passion, increased my income, and paid off my student loans and eventually my house. Best of all, I fell in love with what I did. Today, my main business is The Happy PharmD, which helps pharmacists create inspiring careers and lives. I discovered my sweet spot, one where I love the pharmacy profession again. I teach, train, consult, and coach pharmacists toward a more fulfilling career path at *TheHappyPharmD.com*. I share my knowledge with hundreds of pharmacists to help them start businesses, pursue new career paths, and follow their passions. Hmm... helping others achieve the life and career they want on their terms—now *that* was work that felt admirable, *that* was the book I wanted to write. Let me first be clear what this book *isn't* about. This book isn't about a specific career path. There is no right path to suggest. You could find happiness getting into sales or IT or hospital or management or consulting or entrepreneurship or leaving the pharmacy profession. If you don't know what career path to take, we provide some strategies to discover your path in section four. This book isn't about the best resume, LinkedIn, or interview strategies. I share those strategies in my uber career course called Career Jumpstart. This step-by-step book is for those pharmacists serious about making moves into their next career. You can check out my webinar masterclass that introduces the core concepts of the indispensable pharmacist career here: *www.indispensablepharmacist.com.*

This book isn't going to suggest tacky career strategies, like checking Indeed every day, because those jobs, even the bottom-of-the-barrel ones, get over 100 applications each. This book isn't about telling you where the next best job opportunities are. Opportunities constantly change. Rather, this book will focus on strategies that have stood the test of time. This book will help you discover new paths to become an *indispensable* pharmacist. As you follow the steps to become an indispensable pharmacist, you will naturally find your niche in the marketplace. This book is about discovering what you are excellent at and using it to make your pharmacy career more fulfilling to YOU or turning it into a new career or business, if that's what you want. It's about distilling the lessons I learned after coaching hundreds of pharmacists into indispensable careers. It's about sharing the hard life lessons I learned from spending over $40,000 on my own career development from coaches, conferences, and courses. It's about creating freedom in your life and recognizing that you're in the driver's seat of your career. *Indispensable* is about forging the path you want and not accepting the path laid before you.

I hope you like it and share it with others.

HOW TO USE THIS BOOK

Don't read this book in one sitting. Read this book as though you and I are having a face-to-face conversation. Use the PDF handouts to record your thoughts as you read: *www.indispensablepharmacist.com.*

Answer the questions honestly.

Do the action steps.

Don't skip ahead.

Keep track of your growth. Share this book with a friend. Exchange this book to gain an accountability partner.

Give this book to someone who might need it.

And finally:

Tell the truth about *who you are* and *what you want.* Don't be ashamed to say you hate your job or that you're looking for a new one. Don't settle for mediocre. You spent too much of your time, money, and energy to not LOVE what you do on a daily basis. Write down your goals. Let others see it. You may end up inspiring them.

In the interest of "walking my talk," I'll open this book with one of my most inconvenient truths.

I'M A TERRIBLE
PHARMACIST

Not every student becomes a great pharmacist, and I'm one of those examples. My story starts with how I entered the profession—or rather, how I fell into pharmacy and didn't climb out. I never had much interest in pharmacy in high school, but I liked the idea of going into the medical field. Math and science came naturally to me, and a job in healthcare sounded like a safe, respectable career path—one that wouldn't cause too much trouble for me in the long run. Plus, unlike doctors and nurses, pharmacists don't have to touch blood, butts, or guts. (I still consider that one of the profession's strongest upsides.)

Pharmacy paid well. It allowed people to go "part-time" to focus on family and other pursuits (or so I thought). There were plenty of jobs (back in 2005), according to all the articles foretelling the need for more, more, more PharmDs in the years to come, and my parents nodded approvingly when I mentioned the idea. Besides, I needed to pick a major. Why not take the path of least resistance? And so I became a pharmacist. It never occurred to me that I would be a terrible one.

I'm a terrible pharmacist because I don't have the qualities a typical pharmacist should have.

I lack attention to detail and hate scouring through notes looking for information. Reviewing a patient's chart is a chore rather than a joy.

I'm not a serious person. Let's not even go into how I approach patient care. I've been told, "You need to speak to your patients with more seriousness," more times than I can count.

I'm naturally absent-minded. The simplest things pass by without me noticing, like taxes or a friend's birthday. I've been told that on first impression I come off as though I don't care about others.

I hate professionalism. Now, don't get me wrong: I'm not saying I hate being respectful (in fact, I think the workplace needs a bit more of that), but buttoned-up, "there's a checklist for everything" micromanagement has made the job so dull. I like to experiment and try new things (a no-no in pharmacy). Finally, I practice pharmacy without much interest in the outcome. I care about my patients, but my job doesn't wake me up in the morning with excitement. Helping people lose weight can be fun, but lowering A1c is about as exciting as watching a slideshow of someone else's family vacation. Sadly, these character traits are things that I cannot improve.

I'm a terrible pharmacist because I don't like to do clinical pharmacy activities.

I don't love using medications to help patients solve their problems. In fact, I think the USA has a prescription addiction. Lectures on new drugs bore me to tears; it's difficult enough to get me to sit still for an hour-long CE.

I don't like pharmacy conventions. Well, no, that's not exactly true. I enjoy going to the events because I get to meet people and see friends. What bores are the dreadful presentations. It's like transitioning from playing your favorite game to being forced to sit through an algebra lesson.

I don't pore over pharmacy literature or keep up with the latest and greatest in pharmacology. I hardly know the newer medications, and, if I'm honest, I don't care about learning more. **In short, I feel like a fake PharmD.**

I despise our current healthcare system that rewards the unhealthy.

I despise the treatment of community pharmacists.

I despise the lack of job opportunities for pharmacists.

I despise the fact that "part-time" actually means "you've been demoted."

I despise that it's so difficult for pharmacists to become entrepreneurs. Most of all, I hate seeing how the industry uses, abuses, burns outs, chews up, spits out, and otherwise makes really awesome people miserable. But while I have little interest in practicing the pharmacy profession, I am passionate about pharmacists. This book and my website, *TheHappyPharmD.com*, were born out of my passion for helping pharmacists create fulfilling careers.

Now, you may be wondering, why in the world should you listen to a self-proclaimed terrible pharmacist? But here's what you don't know:

- Because of my pursuits into entrepreneurship, I've received 30 job offers in the last four years. These include traditional jobs like part-time work, pharma jobs, and academia, but also non-traditional jobs like medical writing, independent pharmacy consulting, speaking, and consulting work for companies outside of healthcare.

- I have invested over $40,000 into job strategies and career coaching, and have benefited from them in ways I could never have imagined. I created five businesses. Three failed, but all contributed to my family paying off over $200,000 debts within five years after residency. I coached over 300 pharmacists to help them obtain their career goals.

- My career development articles on Pharmacy Times, DocCafe, Doximity, The Happy PharmD, and Pharmacy School HQ have been viewed over 3.5 million times. While I will never become a leading expert in a specialized field of pharmacy care, I've positioned myself as a niche expert in career development and business.

- I'm a million times happier than I was before.

The work I do now, like writing this book, is the stuff I love to do. In this way, I feel like I'm being the best pharmacist possible: by teaching, coaching and speaking on subjects I care about, like pharmacist burnout and career fatigue. I'm my best self when I help others reach their fullest potential—and that's what I hope *Indispensable* will do for you. Throughout this book,

I want you to discover fulfilling work, even if it's outside of pharmacy, and work in your unique ability, where your work meets your passion, interest, love, strengths, and character. I want you to be happy. I want you to feel in control of your career.

If you don't think it's possible to find work that makes you happy, then this book isn't for you. If you believe you can, then get ready.

This book is split into four parts:

- **Part One** will help you understand our current pharmacy reality and diagnose the source of your unhappiness.

- **Part Two** is about discovering your options and where (and how) you might make a change, whether it's in a new field of pharmacy or outside the profession.

- **Part Three** dives into the messy middle: the strategy behind your career transition.

- **Part Four** focuses on how to make your career indispensable: create value and build valuable relationships.

What you'll have at the end of this book is a new direction—the one you choose. Not only that, but you'll have the necessary tools to build your most valuable asset: your career and living a life by design. But before we can start exploring where you'll go, we need to understand where you are now. Let's take a good, hard look at what we're up against.

PART ONE

DAVID, MEET GOLIATH

When Melissa took her pharmacy job, she felt like she had made a smart decision. Her manager was friendly, her commute was short, and, since a company with a nationally recognized name owned the pharmacy, she felt good about her job security. She was excited to join the team, learn a thing or two, and help her patients. Unfortunately, it didn't take long for Melissa to realize that her day-to-day work was nothing like she imagined. In fact, her job seemed to be getting worse. Slowly but consistently, management peeled away privileges, benefits, and respect and piled more responsibilities onto her workload. It was all Melissa could do to get her work done on time. "I felt like a runner without a finish line," she told me. Fatigued, stressed, and frustrated, Melissa worried that she would burn out.

She brought her concerns to management a couple of times, but their responses were tepid at best and dismissive at worst: they'd just nod their head in agreement and say things like, "We know it's a problem, and we'd like to fix it," and, "Please focus on your goals and objectives." Melissa worried that it would be just a matter of time before a problem occurred—something she or one of her colleagues could be liable for—not because of her lack of ability, but because the workplace environment was leading her to make a mistake.

Thoughts like, "I should try to get another job," started to creep into Melissa's mind but she argued them away with self-doubt and "realistic" thinking. "I told myself that no one else would hire me," she told me during our first consultation, "and that I needed to stick it out and build my experience more. Or maybe I need to get a certification for a company to notice me." I asked her whether she felt trapped in her job, and she didn't hesitate to respond. "Absolutely." Melissa stuck it out and continued to wear herself down. She came home each night exhausted, mentally and physically. Her partner didn't notice the changes immediately but over time could see how Melissa was a shell of who she once was.

Melissa was burned out. Maybe you are, too.

I'd like to pause for a moment because I want you to assess yourself. Are you burned out?

ARE YOU BURNED OUT?

Awareness of the problem is the first step to recovery. Burnout is no exception. Let's first look at how burnout is defined, note the common symptoms, and discuss what it feels like to be burned out. This subject could easily become another book and increasingly academic, but I promise this will be short and painless.

Research on burnout in pharmacists is present, but not prevalent. The American Pharmacist Association performed a survey reviewing pharmacists' outlooks on their job, and just over 50% considered quitting their jobs (J Am Pharm Assoc (2003). 2013 May-Jun;53(3):282-96). A recent survey (at time of this publication) published in the *Journal of Hospital Pharmacists* found 61.2% of pharmacists presented one burnout symptom (Hosp Pharm. 2017 Dec;52(11):742-751).

Oddly enough, community pharmacist burnout data is sparse. The pharmacy job niche every pharmacist knows where burnout is most significant.

According to leading burnout researcher Christina Maslach, the three elements that define job burnout are emotional exhaustion, lack of personal accomplishment, and cynicism or detachment.

Emotional Exhaustion

You know that feeling you get when you're with in-laws for too long? Well, that's how you feel all the time. Each interaction with a patient, colleague, or manager creates stress, induces anxiety, and leaves you feeling depleted. You feel like you don't have any more to give. Emotional exhaustion caused by the workplace leads to a life where you feel like you never are fully rested. The weekend comes, but the dread of returning to work steals any relaxation you earned. Justine, a burned-out pharmacist, described her life like this: "I would request three-day weekends, but even though I felt physically recharged, my mind would spend spare moments dreading and worrying about my next workday."

Symptoms of emotional exhaustion:

- Anger—A normal emotion, but it quickly surfaces at work, and in later stages more often around those you love most.

- Anxiety—Not the normal kind of worry; a physical and emotional state of always being on edge.

- Chronic fatigue—In the beginning of your work, you may feel constantly tired. But over time this feeling turns into emotional and physical dread of work.

- Depression—Feelings of sadness without direct causation, experiencing extreme guilt or worthlessness. You may consider the world better without you. (Seek immediate help if you feel this way. For the National Suicide Prevention Lifeline, call 1-800-273-8255).

- Lack of focus—You may find yourself forgetting important things like taxes, a close friend's birthday, or turning off the stove before leaving your house. Your work may be piling up and causing you further anxiety.

- Loss of appetite—Early on, you may find yourself so distracted that you'll skip meals. Later, you could find yourself not fitting into your pants because of lost weight.

- Insomnia—From trouble falling asleep to just not being able to sleep at all, insomnia is a common occurrence. Illness—You may observe yourself becoming ill more often. Your body is telling you your stress is more than it can handle

- Physical symptoms—Chest pain, dizziness, fainting, gastrointestinal pain, headaches, heart palpitations, and shortness of breath (all of which should be medically assessed).

Lack of Personal Accomplishment

"I felt like I was running full sprints without a finish line."

Lack of personal accomplishment feels like you are given tasks that will never be completed. You're told, "Run," without there being any indication of when you can stop. You're on a proverbial hamster wheel of work. Clock in, run the wheel, clock out. Nothing changes. Work feels meaningless, leaving you empty at the end of the day.

Symptoms of lack of personal accomplishments:

- Apathy—You ask yourself at work, "What's the point?" but never really answer the question, because the truth is too scary to face. Enhanced irritability—You have had enough of the bureaucracy, politics, and management that stop you from doing what you were meant to do. Every time you receive an email from your manager, you curse and complain to coworkers.

- Poor performance—It's not you; it's the system, right? There is no way for you to escape out of the impossible metrics management creates. Your performance has either slowly decreased, or you may be a shell of your former performance from when you were green.

Cynicism or Detachment

Work doesn't mean anything to the cynic. Maybe it once did, but the cynic would be happy if no one ever bothered her again at work. That's the key word, "bother." Interactions are never seen in a positive light. Every interaction is burdened by a negative outlook. "What does this person want from me?" rather than, "How can I help?"

Detachment is a lack of empathy, compassion, and general feeling toward the job. A detached worker wouldn't waste more than a few seconds thinking about a patient who recently died. If a coworker unexpectedly dies, the first thing that would come to mind to a detached worker would be, "Now I have to pick up her workload."

Signs of cynicism or detachment:

- Detachment—You find yourself just not caring about others. You couldn't care less about what happens to your patients, coworkers, or colleagues. It's not because you don't want to care, but it's a process of becoming detached from those around you. You may call in sick often, consistently come to work late, or ignore clear directives from your manager.

- Isolation—Maybe you think you're just introverted. But the truth is you've been ignoring social interaction more and more over time. You ignore personal social invites. Later, you find yourself becoming angry by simple requests from others.

- Loss of enjoyment—At first, you accept that work will not satisfy you. There's nothing that will make you feel fulfilled at work. Over time, you will create ways to avoid doing work. This effect will trickle down to the simplest of tasks, even outside of work. A loved one may ask you to do something easy, and the request can set ablaze your anger.

- Pessimism—Glass half empty isn't enough to define the way you naturally think and speak. You are naturally negative about positive statements or predictions. This book may sound like a load of garbage to you. After hearing a hopeful comment, you are quick to shut down that hope, because you believe there isn't any hope left.

If you feel these symptoms, you may be burned out. If you think, "Well, I only have a few of these symptoms. And they don't occur all the time." Be warned. You are experiencing the first symptoms of burnout. These symptoms will escalate if you do not take action.

After reading these symptoms, you may feel convinced you are burned out, or you may still feel skeptical. If you'd like to know whether or not you're truly burned out, you can complete Maslach's Burnout Inventory. Christina Maslach dedicated her life to the research of job burnout. From her decades of research, she created a survey that predicts a person's level of burnout. Specifically, you can take the MBI-Human Services Survey, a test for professionals in any service industry.

WHAT ARE THE RESULTS OF A BURNED-OUT LIFESTYLE?

Here is an email I received from a widow of a pharmacist:

[Dear Alex,]

"This evening I read your article about the top five reasons for pharmacist burn out. I was saddened by your article because it tells the story of my husband's life as a pharmacist. Sadly, he recently passed away at age 57. He had never had any health problems but was extremely stressed by his job. Shortly after his death, a coworker sobbed to me, "[Company Name] killed him. You will never convince me otherwise." I struggle to deal with his untimely death, knowing that he stuck with the job because of student loans and four children to support. He did his best to hide the stress from me. I hope your article will be read by pharmacists in similar situations and will help them in some way. Regina Scott"

If you feel like your burnout symptoms are manageable, let me assure you that Regina's husband felt the same way. Here's what Regina had to share after I asked her if I could share her story:

"I hope that you will tell Kent's story, and I hope that some good will come of it. Mostly I hope that someone with the power will change what is wrong with the pharmacy profession so other life stories won't have the same ending as Kent's.

"Thank you for what you are doing to help other pharmacists. I wish you great success and hope that some day pharmacy will be an enjoyable and rewarding career as it was when Kent started."

Pharmacists' lives are literally being cut short.

I conducted my own research on the subject of pharmacist suicide. Unfortunately, the current data is lacking. To my surprise, I found the CDC NOMS (National Occupational Mortality Survey) program. This database tracks cause of death and occupation. What I found may trouble you.

Out of 482 occupations, pharmacists hold the **14th-highest suicide risk**.

When compared to the general public, **pharmacists are twice as likely to commit suicide**.

You can read my research in this blog post: *https://www.thehappypharmd.com/pharmacist-suicide-risk-what-we-know-and-dont-know/*.

My hope is you will get serious about developing your career, because suicide is a possibility for anyone.

If you feel like suicidal ideation is a part of normal life, please contact the suicide prevention hotline (National Suicide Prevention Lifeline. Call 1-800-273-8255).

You cannot afford to stay in a job you hate. Your life is too precious to waste on a company that values the bottom line more than your life, or for the profession of pharmacy.

Kent's story isn't unique. Anyone is capable of repeating his choice. If you don't create an indispensable career, suicide is a possibility. While I believe your life is of the utmost importance, your quality of life is also at stake. What is more likely to occur is a life of disappointment, frustration, and unfulfillment. But this life still holds consequences.

A burned-out lifestyle has negative emotional, physical, and relational impact. Your life cannot include emotional room for others. People's problems seem too big for you to solve or even think about. You can't imagine helping others outside of work, where you're forced to constantly solve problems for others. Helping a close friend move into their home isn't an act of love, it's now a burden. You may grow distant from your friends and colleagues. You find your friends don't want to talk to you as much as they once did. Why, you ask? Well, who wants to hear someone complain about work all the time? They just don't understand you. "Cheer up," they say. "Aren't you making six figures?" They just don't understand.

Your family no longer brings you the joy you hope for. In fact, close friends may say something to you like, "You're making six figures. How bad can it be?" You find yourself agitated by the simplest requests from your children or partner. Your spouse encourages you to look for another job, but he doesn't understand our pharmacy job market, the saturation, the difficulties, or the challenges. You feel stuck, and not even your closest loved ones are in the same prison. Besides the obvious personal consequences of burnout mentioned above in the symptoms section, one literature review from 2017 found "Burnout was a significant predictor of the following physical consequences: hypercholesterolemia, type 2 diabetes, coronary heart disease, hospitalization due to cardiovascular disorder, musculoskeletal pain, changes in pain experiences, prolonged fatigue, headaches, gastrointestinal issues, respiratory problems, severe injuries and mortality below the age of 45 years. The psychological effects were insomnia, depressive symptoms, use of psychotropic and antidepressant medications, hospitalization for mental disorders and psychological ill-health symptoms. Job dissatisfaction, absenteeism, new disability pension, job demands, job resources and presenteeism were identified as professional outcomes." (PLoS One. 2017; 12(10): e0185781).

Your burnout-inducing job isn't worth your life or a poor quality of life. Now is the time to change.

WHAT CAN YOU DO ABOUT IT?

"Why change anything? No one will give you a chance," you think, alone in your burned-out prison. Burned-out behavior breeds an inactive career. Your curiosity about pharmacy is squelched. After coming home from a tiresome day, you don't find the positive energy to build a new career. You justify your remaining hours to be spent on entertainment because you've had an awful day.

Career development is usually the last thing a burned-out pharmacist wishes to do. How can a burned-out pharmacist become indispensable? There's so much stacked against you, right?

I've read many articles about burnout. The stats are discouraging. But what's sadder is the advice offered to burned-out pharmacists.

The recommendations are things like:

- Look at the bright side.

- Ask for a different schedule.

- Try to work things out with your manager.

- Petition for a location transfer.

- Request more technician help.

- Well, at least you have a reliable job.

And of course…

It could always be worse.

What they really ought to be saying is: "Maybe it's time for you to do something different. What types of jobs interest you?"

The best way to relieve burnout is to quit the job that's burning you out. It isn't rocket science; no double-blind placebo control trial is necessary. Quit that stressful job and the burnout will go away. But many don't feel like leaving is an option. What keeps unhappy PharmDs trapped?

Be forewarned. The next few chapters call out what's wrong with pharmacy and the trappings of a financially safe lifestyle. Some of the issues may resonate in your current situation, while others you may disagree with—and that's fine. What's true about lifestyle choices for others may not be true for you (and vice-versa). I've also included caveats for each aspect because good things can come from awful situations, and I don't want you to read the following problems and feel like there is no getting out. There is.

I've helped hundreds of unhappy PharmDs take steps toward finding or creating a more fulfilling path, and our work always starts with the same question: Why are you looking for help? We'll start with the answer I hear most often.

S-T-U-C-K

People outside of our profession often ask me: "Why are pharmacists so unhappy?" I reply with a question: "Have you ever felt trapped for an extended period?" Sometimes people can relate and offer an empathetic example, and other times they confess that they, too, feel stuck. The honest (lucky) ones reply with, "Not really." So I explain it to them: Being a pharmacist can feel as though you're trapped. **Management does not care.** Your manager doesn't have your back. Upper management makes decisions you think are more aligned with "profit care" or "number care," a concept we'll be discussing shortly, rather than health care. You feel like your leaders have hung you out to dry. Your boss may listen to complaints and respond with a little corporate rhetoric, but nothing changes. It's like they want you to fail at your job.

The people we serve do not care. On top of this, your patients have no patience. While, of course, the vast majority of those who step up to your counter are polite (or at least civil), the rude ones can ruin your whole day. They demand their medications immediately and blame you for their problems. You feel more like an employee at corporate assembly line than a DOCTOR of pharmacy. "Hello, welcome to McPharmacy, how may I help you?" Patients seem unaware that you are a doctor. Some people don't even know hospitals have pharmacies. **Your coworkers feel the same.** Your coworkers are just as miserable (and miserable to be around) as you. I have felt the wrath of a bully manager and bully coworkers. I've been let down by unreliable colleagues who create more work through their inattentiveness and laziness, by unreliable technicians who make the job harder rather than easier, and broken promises from management. The onslaught of disrespect comes from all sides. Everyone is unhappy, and it only compounds in what feels like a prison of professionals and technicians.

Your colleagues blame you for everything. Nurses, doctors, PAs, NPs, dentists, and everyone else in between can't believe you're making their jobs more difficult. "Why can't you just approve the script?" they demand. Your job is to make sure medications are safe for patients, but the medical team and the patient don't seem to care about that; they just want you to hand over the drug. Every pharmacist can tell a similar story—but rarely do I meet a PharmD who feels like she can walk away. Whether it's school debt, the job market, fear of failure, or family considerations, leaving the job doesn't feel like an option.

After I explain this, the stranger typically looks at me wide-eyed and says, "I had no idea." And to that, I reply, "Most non-pharmacists don't." The culture of pharmacy and the mindset it drills into its pharmacists is a unique beast.

A Financial Prison

While there are a number of reasons PharmDs feel stuck in their unhappy jobs, the biggest by far is the school debt they're working to pay off. Academia has the USA by the gonads. Currently, Americans owe $1.48 trillion in student loans, and the average student loan for the graduating pharmacist in 2017 was $163,494, according to the AACP report.

When I speak with students, I can feel and hear their angst. They're starting their careers in a financial hole—and they know that hole will only get deeper. School debt claims its percentage of every paycheck, and then rent, the car payment, credit card balances, and eating three times a day take their share. After doing a residency or picking their first job, young professionals are encouraged to buy a home (whether by family or culture), and likely double their loans, locking themselves into another $1,000 to $3,000 monthly payment. On top of this, there are the demands to save for retirement, which take away from their funds to pay off this crippling debt. Here's the flow of the financial trap:

- Graduate

- Crippling student loan debt payments come due

- Seek job to pay off debts

- Buy a home (mortgage payments ranging $1,000 to $3,000+ monthly payments)

- Start a family (further increasing expenses)

- "Forced" to stay a job to pay off loans

- Prolong the time to financial freedom by investing in retirement now (depending on how much investing)

The way I see it, owing thousands a month to loans and other commitments is worse than a trap; it's a financial prison that robs unhappy PharmDs of the freedom to find more fulfilling work. Sadly, most find themselves in a state of financial tug-of-war:

- Wanting to be debt free.

- Wanting to invest now so they can quit ASAP.

- Wanting to quit, but unable to afford their lifestyle.

And the only winner in this story is their employer. Living paycheck to paycheck is no way for a pharmacist to build a valuable career. So, how can a burned-out pharmacist escape from his job when he desperately needs to maintain his expenses?My wise friend Hans Boateng, PharmD MBA, believes you should invest now to reap benefits later. I agree with him, to an extent, but I also think it's important to aggressively pursue a valuable career and financial freedom. If you agree, then you need to decide: which do you want first? Freedom from loan payments to be able to do what you want, or to reap a rich retirement fund 30-40 years from now (perhaps earlier if you follow the FIRE philosophy—financially independent, retire early)? Retirement investment is essential, obviously—I'm a big fan of investing now and did so all during my "miserable" job—but I used the majority of my income to eliminate debts so that one day, if I wanted to, I could quit my job. And yes, that meant sacrificing some creature comforts, but my financial freedom was a bigger priority than going out to dinner.

Today, my monthly expenses equate to about $2,200 per month. Our house is paid off, student loans are gone, there's no car payment, and we have a six-month emergency fund. I quit my traditional pharmacy job (with a pension) in August 2018, and I haven't looked back. My business creates more than enough to cover my monthly expenses, so I now have a lot more money to invest for retirement.

The lesson here is that, no matter how daunting it may feel to think about leaving your job or seeking a new career path, you do have options. You can take action today to break yourself out of the trap. **You're not stuck**.

SIT DOWN AND SHUT UP

My first "real" job had me so excited. After completing my residency, I was hired as a Primary Care Pharmacy Specialist. Boy, I loved that title. My whole life had led to this big moment, and it felt like all the work I'd done had finally paid off. In some ways, my hiring came as a surprise since I had a lot of things working against me:

- I only completed a one-year residency

- I was late to apply for the job

- I didn't know the manager of the pharmacy

- They wanted someone with hepatitis experience (which I didn't have)

I still don't understand why they picked me, but I am happy they did. I wouldn't be where I am today without the unpleasant experience that came next. My first few months on the job were filled with... nothing. There were no other Primary Care Pharmacists on site. I asked for projects, volunteered for things, and tried to fill my time with productive work, but I felt like my manager blocked my progress at every turn. My assigned mentor, who worked 100 miles away from me at a smaller site, wasn't any help, either. I didn't realize it immediately, but she wasn't an Alex Barker fan (there are quite a few, and rightly so; I've been a stinker for years). My personality seemed to clash with hers, and no matter how many times I apologized (for things I didn't necessarily think were wrong), I couldn't win her over. Slowly but surely, my manager (another Alex Barker hater) directed me to work in the anticoagulation clinic. I wasn't thrilled about the move, but I was happy to be doing patient care. I took the job on eagerly and made the best of it. I later found out I had been moved into the anticoag clinic was because my mentor persuaded my manager that I didn't belong in primary care. Unfortunately, my troubles only got worse from there. I hadn't been officially approved for patient care. Like all new employees, I had to undergo a trial period of peer review before I could become an independent provider—and mine didn't go well. My mentor would berate me over my notes and patient interactions. I felt stupid. I would go home dejected and wake up the next day anxious over what my mentor would say to me. I began to worry whether I would keep my job. My manager would call me into her office and scold me over trivial issues. I dreaded answering her phone calls or opening her emails because I knew something awful was coming my way. I felt like my career was in my manager's hands, and she seemed to want to crush my spirit at every opportunity. At the time, I have to admit that I didn't have much of a backbone and rarely stood up for myself, something I regret today. But a part of me said, "Sit down and shut up. How can you be complaining with how good you have it?" I felt trapped, alone, and helpless, like my career was in ruins and there was nothing I could do about it. A bully in the workplace can drive you to quit your job (even if you enjoy it). It can make you wake up every morning dreading the day ahead, not to mention the amount of stress it creates once you're there. UK pharmacists tracked the rate of reported bullying in pharmacy and noted: "According to figures from the NHS staff survey published in February 2014, 23% of pharmacists had experienced bullying, harassment or abuse from another member of staff in the previous 12 months."[1] That figure is high; much higher than what I wish it were. Twenty-three percent also means that bullying culture is everywhere in pharmacy. It's hard to avoid jerks, but you can avoid companies that employ jerks. You can also choose not to engage in others' toxicity.

Hating Life is Part of the Fun… But It Doesn't Have to Be

Misery loves company, as the saying goes. My mom would tell me all the time, "Be careful about who you hang out with," and, "Who you are attracted to says a lot about you." She still reminds me of that fact occasionally. If your colleagues hate their work, boss, company, or life, then you will, too. If they act like jerks toward other people—even you—then there's a good chance you'll respond in kind. It's only natural to adopt the work ethic, attitude, and culture of those around you. Coworkers complain to each other how much they hate a particular employee, manager, or task, and everyone nods in agreement. Mutually hating someone or something can be a weirdly bonding experience. Unfortunately, hatred rarely leads to positive action.

If you have colleagues who hate their jobs, work, managers, coworkers, or lives, ask yourself this, "Do I want a career like theirs?"Let's move away from toxic pharmacists. **Reject their destructive way of thinking and don't engage in their bullying behavior.** Think of it as an opportunity to "be the change you want to see" in the pharmacy world and one small step toward improving its culture.

FEAR, LOATHING, AND MICROMANAGEMENT

Autonomy is key to a healthy career (and a healthy life). When you feel in control of your job and your decisions and you are confident that your managers have your back, you're more likely to grow within your role. It certainly feels a lot better than the alternative. Pharmacists are trained to be somewhat paranoid. We don't like it when things get out of control, when systems fail, or when there isn't a clear answer. Our control culture inevitably creates a few micromanaging bosses, which invariably leads to an unhappy workplace. Having a micromanager for a boss makes you feel like you have no autonomy and drains you of any creative energy. When I worked for a micromanager, I came home exhausted every day. I would sit on my couch and tell my wife, Megan, "Honey, I need to just sit here for an hour. Can you take care of the girls, please?" I needed time to recuperate. Otherwise, I found myself snapping at my kids or Meg. Micromanagers suck souls dry and make the trapped pharmacist feel worse. When you give your best energy to your job and receive a constant barrage of negative comments, demanding statements, and even bullying remarks in return, you can't possibly build a valuable career. Instead, your mindset starts to shift. You become fearful, convinced that one misstep would mean disaster.

The F Word

The fear of failure is hardwired into our profession. There's a good reason for that, of course: if a pharmacist messes up, someone could get hurt or even die. Six-plus years of schooling beat it into us that failure is not an option. If you fail, then you can't graduate. If you miss something on the job, someone gets hurt. The guidelines and expectations in the workplace are equally strict. If you fail, then you don't have a job anymore. Worse, you may end up getting sued (a truly gut-wrenching experience) or losing your license. The message is clear: failures can't work in pharmacy. So let me get this straight. As a pharmacist, I am expected to be 100% on top of my game, stay up-to-date on advancements, and be ready to answer any questions a patient might have... but I'm not allowed to explore anything new or experimental, expand my knowledge through trial and error, or learn from experience. Okay.

If you DO misstep as a pharmacist, scrutiny is your reward. A mistake on the job is met with punishment, reprimands, and write-ups. Some receive increased micromanagement and PIPs (performance improvement plans), as I did. More often than not, I hear pharmacists complain about their managers creating impossible PIPs and setting unreasonable expectations. They suspect their bosses have set them up to fail. Pharmacist Reddit forums have pages upon pages dedicated to pharmacists explaining their unjust situations. Setting aside the micromanagement and bad bosses, think about the mindset a PharmD might have in that situation.

- I'll never do it right. Why try?

- I'm stuck here.

- How can I advance now?

- That's what I get for sticking my neck out.

- This is impossible.

The mindset that derives from such an unforgiving (not to mention unrealistic) culture is detrimental to the people expected to be high performers. **Failure is bound to happen**. No human can be perfect at her job. A healthy business recognizes that fact and fosters experimentation and allows its valuable employees to learn from their mistakes.

But pharmacy isn't a healthy business.

HEALTH CARE? TRY "NUMBER CARE"

Many pharmacy companies focus more on their numbers than on their patients. It's a fact felt by thousands of pharmacists every day as they set about meeting their metric goals. Patient care? Only if you have time.

Bryce, a community pharmacist, told me, "My manager scolded me during my annual appraisal because I 'spent too much time with patients.' For my numbers to go up, I had to 'focus only on my goals,' which have nothing to do with patient care!" His experience is the perfect illustration of number care, the profit-first and humans-last machine that the pharmacy industry has become. A company's bottom line is important. Naturally, right? You can't run a business without being profitable. Otherwise, the business closes. But many community pharmacies, hospitals, and health care organizations have become this ugly monster of profit over patients. These organizations battle insurance companies and government regulation for their well-being. The system in place is broken, and many pharmacists agree that their work, at times, places more emphasis on performing better on metrics than on helping individuals. Number care gives pharmacists two choices: comply with management's numerical goals or leave.

Now, I understand the need for measurable goals. While some pharmacists claim they want more patient-centric care in their jobs, "Deliver impactful and life-changing conversations about health" isn't exactly quantifiable. Management needs measurable outcomes for all pharmacies, or they can't improve. I get it.

Unfortunately, these numbered goals take precedence over patient care. Pharmacists feel trapped to meet these outcomes (often out of reach), and a patient's experience or even her safety can fall by the wayside. That is something I have a hard time stomaching and, given that you've picked up this book, I'm willing to bet that you do, too. Nobody chooses to enter an abusive system.

You're not alone if you've felt like your job has become about meeting metric goals over providing care for an individual. You had a desire to join pharmacy at some point because you like helping people. You thought helping people in pharmacy seemed like a good fit based on the job market, your abilities, and what other people told you. The desire to help others is an innate drive, and entire industries have been built around it—but industries have also been built around abusing those they claim to help. Health care is the industry's name, and it's an effective lure for those who want to help others. Sadly, those who enter the pharmacy profession for all the right reasons get chewed up before they see the number care machine for what it is. Others believe that something far more sinister is at play.

The Conspiracy Theory

Years ago I spoke with Rachel, a pharmacist who wanted out of her retail pharmacy job. Aside from the typical complaints I hear about community pharmacy, such as bad hours and being poorly treated, she said: "Everyone knows pharmacist salaries are going down. Machines will replace us."

Her statement struck me for two reasons. First, the way she said it was very matter-of-fact. Second, Rachel seemed to have accepted that this dire outlook was the inevitable future of pharmacy. Although I disagreed with her sentiment, it made me wonder whether there is a conspiracy at work in the pharmacy industry.

Before we get started, here's a disclaimer: The conspiracy theory that I am about to present to you has not been validated. It is the only product of my analysis of industry trends, my personal experience, and my knowledge of the pharmacy job marketplace. Got it? Okay, let's dive down the ol' rabbit hole.

You probably know that pharmacists are seeing a decrease in job opportunities, slow job growth, lower salaries offered, and flattening pay trends. However, this wasn't the prediction for the future of our industry.

In 2000, the Pharmacy Workforce Center, created by the American Association of Colleges of Pharmacy, released a report stating that there would be a massive demand for pharmacists in twenty years due to rising health care costs and an increase in the aging population. This group tried to read the tea leaves and expected that the future demand for pharmacists would far outpace the supply.

Now, a short eighteen years later, the supply of pharmacists has exceeded the expected demand. This has had multiple effects on the job economy for pharmacists, including:

- Fewer available jobs, especially in urban areas

- Elimination of signing bonuses

- Decreased benefits

- Decreased actual salary/wages

- Decreased offered salary/wages, especially for new graduates

- Increased part-time jobs such as floater positions, for which reduced benefits are offered

- Flatter salaries over a ten- to twenty-year period

Now, every conspiracy theory (or at least the good ones) starts with an important question: Cui bono? Who benefits?

Let's think for a moment about who is benefiting from these changes in the marketplace. Not the pharmacists. Nope. It's the pharmacy executives, business owners, and stockholders.

Allow me to explain: Hiring a pharmacist is a big deal because it costs lots of money. The average salary for a pharmacist is well over $100,000 a year, plus benefits, in any state in the U.S. If you run a retail pharmacy chain or a hospital, the easiest way to boost profits is to create systems that help you eliminate costs—and pharmacists are a HUGE cost.

If you were a pharmacy executive responsible for hiring pharmacists, would you prefer to have more applicants or fewer applicants for your new pharmacy jobs? Of course, you want more applicants. The bigger your applicant pool, the more qualified potential employees you can find and the less you can offer to pay. Why? Well, because more people are desperate for the few available jobs you have, especially if your business is located in a choice area. As a manager, you get to be picky on who you choose. You also need to increase the requirements and preferences to rule out less-than-desirable candidates.

So, is it any wonder why pharmacy executives want more pharmacists in the job marketplace? And thus, the conspiracy theory was born: What if pharmacy executives supported (even financed?) the Pharmacy Workforce Center's 2000 report stating that there will be a huge need for pharmacists in the future? What if there is a bigger reason pharmacy executives support the new pharmacy schools popping up all over the country? What if these new pharmacy schools aren't intended to meet demand, but instead to decrease salaries? Ever wonder why the majority of the jobs offered at pharmacy job conventions at schools are sponsored by major retail pharmacies?

Makes sense, doesn't it?

And if you really want to make the mental leap, the way Rachel did, then ask yourself: If the goal is to decrease salaries, then isn't it just a matter of time before the industry replaces PharmDs with automation?

Personally, I don't believe that robots can replace pharmacists. Innovation is bound to happen, and, yes, it may eliminate the need for a human to do certain jobs, but machines can't replace a human. And let me tell you what I don't like about the "machines are replacing us" argument: it ignores how much control we still have over our careers. No matter what you believe about big pharma, executives, and ivory towers, you should remember that there will always be a need for humans in the marketplace. No matter how many machines are made to perform some of our technical duties, no device can replace the brain of a pharmacist and help people the way a human pharmacist can. PharmDs are indispensable, and that means **you have more agency than you may realize**—but only if you take control of your career.

IT'S TIME TO TAKE CHARGE

Here's your call to action: Don't take this lying down. Whether or not you have all of the problems we discussed in this section, you need to take charge of your career. You should be upset that salaries and benefits for pharmacists are down and full-time jobs are being turned into multiple part-time positions to keep costs low. So, take that emotion and turn it into useful action.

Now is the time for you to take the reins of your career and improve your circumstances. Here are a few ideas to help you get started:

Determine what you want. Here are things you need to decide in the coming chapters. Have you asked for it?

Do a values check. Many pharmacists are unsettled in their work due to the disconnect between the company's core values and their own. But if you don't know what you value, you will struggle to find an employer that matches your passion. **Find what fulfills you.** Professional meetings discuss the latest clinical innovations, new guidelines, and nuances of the profession. But rarely do we consider what's on the mind of the typical pharmacist: How can I find better work in this profession? This book won't aim to answer this question, but rather a more important one: How can I make my work more fulfilling?

Identify your unique ability. This is the first step toward making yourself indispensable.

Connect with like-minded people. You're not alone in this fight. There are other pharmacists, including me, who want others to succeed. In fact, the only way you'll make a successful transition in or out of pharmacy is with the help of others. **Decide whether you will stay.** I'm not convinced that everyone who joined the profession should continue the pharmacy career. I believe some pharmacists are great entrepreneurs, franchise owners, side hustlers, real estate brokers, writers, speakers—the list could go on forever. What feels right to you?

We'll be diving into all of these questions in Part Two. I'll show you how to discover your options and make them a reality, whether it's in a new company, a new field of pharmacy, or outside the profession. I hope you're ready to do the work.

PART TWO

FIND YOUR PATH

They say every journey begins with a single step—in fact, "they" have said it so many times that I wouldn't be surprised if you rolled your eyes when you read those words. And while, yes, the phrase has been used in a thousand different iterations in everything from diet plans to whiskey ads, it endures because it's true. You have to start somewhere.

Can you think of one small thing you can do today or tomorrow that will make you feel a little happier when you show up to work? Here are a few examples to get you started:

- Volunteer for the on-the-job activity you enjoy most. Give a coworker a compliment.

- Volunteer for a cause you care about.

- Pick a common complaint at work and spend ten minutes trying to fix the problem.

- Tell yourself a cheesy affirmation.

- Ask for a raise! Think of this small act as a declaration and a promise: **starting today, you will move toward happiness on the job—and from happiness, you can find fulfillment.** It's time to take that first step toward making yourself indispensable.

As I mentioned earlier, I initially wrote this book as an honest look at the pharmacy workplace and a how-to for creating a valuable career within it. But as I explored my career's journey and those of my clients, I found that limiting your scope only to pharmacy significantly limits your potential. What about the pharmacist who feels called to be creative through drawing or photography? What about the pharmacist who loves system management and wants to improve the corporate system structure? What about the pharmacist who loves patient interactions, but hates the documentation?

Indispensability, I realized, goes way beyond the walls of the pharmacy. More than anything else, it is about **creating value for others**. That could mean creating value for your current employer, or for your own clients through the company you start. It could mean creating value within your community through service or a creative side hustle. There are a lot of ways you can be indispensable, and your path to finding how will be a mix of the following:

- Curiosity

- Your unique ability

- Ikigai

- Opportunity

Let's discover together what you need to create an indispensable career.

CURIOSITY, PLAY, AND JOY

If you watch enough interviews of "successful" people, you may notice a trend. Ask how they got their start and you'll hear things like:

> I found myself obsessed with the idea.

> I devoured every book I could get my hands on. Nobody was talking about it, so I started researching. I wanted to see what was inside, so I cracked it open and started tinkering.

> I could have never predicted my career path.

> No one else will look out for you besides yourself.

Big things, whether we're talking about success, innovation, or even learning the piano, start with curiosity.

Michael Jordan's older brother Larry was his basketball rival and role model. Michael chose his famous number 23 because it was (roughly) half of Larry's number 45 and, as he shared in his autobiography, Michael hoped to be half as good as his brother. (It's safe to say he achieved that goal.) MJ's obsession with basketball started off as a curiosity; he wanted to know more about this sport his brother loved. The rest is history. "Okay, Alex," you might be thinking, "but Michael Jordan is one of the greatest athletes of all time. How does this apply to me?"

Each person's curiosity starts from the same place: a question. Michael thought, "How could I become half the player my brother is?" Your natural curiosity creates questions every day.

What is that?

How does it work?

Can we make it better?

Is there an easier way to verify prior authorizations?

Could I provide medication therapy management outside my organization?Can I change the code of our system's EMR?Would that company hire me to consult for them?

Could I get paid to write?

At one point in your life, you wondered if you could become a pharmacist—and maybe there's a bit of career magic in that question. What was it about pharmacy that intrigued you? What about pharmacy still intrigues you? What do you wish you knew more about or understood better? Is there something in your current job that makes you even a little curious? The answers to these questions may drive you in a new direction, or you could realize you're right where you want to be and just need to make some tweaks. What new things could you try this week to satisfy your curiosity? What might they lead you to discover?

Your natural curiosity should lead you to new opportunities in (or out of) the pharmacy profession. I know former pharmacists who now work in finance, tech consulting, blockchain technology, and real estate; one is an author, another is a website builder, and another is a facility manager. Each of them followed their curiosity to places they never expected when they started. Your curiosity could do the same for you.

So, what happened to it? Where is it now? If you're in a job that offers no room for autonomy and no space for creativity, you've likely lost track of your curiosity. If that's where you are today, take note: **you can find it again**.

Rediscover Your Curiosity

Your brain is hardwired for curiosity. When you were little, no one had to tell you to be curious. You had an innate desire to learn, and it led you to discover things you liked and were exceptionally good at doing. It was most likely the driving force behind your obsession with space, or dinosaurs, or playing a sport, or your favorite school subject. Years later, your curiosity drove you to pursue a career in pharmacy and, coupled with your natural ability, it kept you there. So, where did it all go wrong? What happened to your curiosity about pharmacy, and is it even possible to get it back?

In a word, yes. And I recommend you start where your interests and abilities intersect. Consider the story of the Animal School by George Reavis: a school where ducks and squirrels and eagles and rabbits gathered to study the same curriculum. Duck was great at swimming, but terrible at running. As a result, he had to drop his swimming class to focus his efforts on running. Rabbit was a great runner, but he crumbled under the make-up work he was assigned in swimming class. Eagle was constantly in trouble because he refused to climb trees and insisted on flying instead. None of the animals excelled because they were forced to hone skills they weren't interested in rather than perfecting their natural gifts. Like the animals in the story, you have natural gifts and abilities that distinguish you from those around you, but when you're in a job that squashes those, your motivation can disappear. The key to firing it back up is to find ways to express your talents.

My youngest daughter, Addilyn, is at her best when she's singing and dancing. She's brave, rebellious, and boisterous, and she loves to do her own thing. No one has to remind her to sing and dance. You couldn't stop her from it if you tried. Most kids are that way. They do what comes naturally, and certain activities automatically draw them in. When I was young, I loved being in the spotlight, and I loved school because I got a lot of attention. (My detention records prove I was willing to do just about anything for an audience.) I had a strong, confident voice, and I didn't hesitate to use it. My public speaking ability and willingness to ham it up now and then are natural strengths, and standing up in front of a crowd is something I love to do—so I got curious: **how could I put those things to work for me**?

At the intersection of my interest and ability, during my fourth year of pharmacy school, I discovered a passion for teaching and employed it to teach nursing students about medications. In the years that followed, my desire to help people and my public speaking skill led me to numerous teaching opportunities in a variety of settings. And it all started with a little reflection, some curiosity, and a willingness to try new things.

But I'm not Curious About Anything

"I don't think I like pharmacy at all. I don't think there's any hope for me." Tough words to hear from Pooja, a chain store pharmacist in the Carolinas. I believe many pharmacists find themselves in the same situation as Pooja: uncurious about pharmacy. If you aren't curious, it's time to dig deep. Let me show you how a simple curiosity turned into an obsession for me. Then we'll dive into how Pooja rediscovered a hidden curiosity, and how it created the opportunity for her next job.

When I was a child, I loved to pretend. My childhood was spent pretending I was a superhero, or my Legos were at war, or my beanie babies were secret agents. I eventually squelched my pretending habit because it wasn't socially acceptable by about seventh grade. My interests turned to more "appropriate" outlets like WWE, video games, and home movies. It wasn't until I was 30 that I returned to my pretending habit. Recently, I started playing Dungeons and Dragons with my friends. If you aren't familiar with the nerdy game, the rules are simple: you pretend you're a fantasy character who can do anything you want. A friend asked me if I ever thought about playing it before, and I initially said no and yes. You see, I've always been a nerd, but I could always say, "Well, at least I don't play Dungeons and Dragons." I didn't want to cross that line, but now I'm thrilled I did. My friends and I pretend together a fantastical and hilarious story as we battle dragons, goblins, and our wills. By the end of the night, my stomach is sore from laughter. I would never have experienced this great joy if I didn't entertain the idea of where my curiosity lies. I knew that deep down I had an interest in the game, but social norms held me back from trying. I threw aside those

73

norms and accepted a new identity: a man who pretends. Back to Pooja. She was convinced that pharmacy didn't hold a place for her anymore. So I had Pooja do a simple curiosity exercise. I asked Pooja to set aside at least an hour for time alone. This was a free writing exercise, and didn't want her kids or anything else distracting from this. First, I asked Pooja to write down this phrase: "Write drunk." Why? Pharmacists are usually left-brain people, we focus on the details and use logical reasoning. But creativity and curiosity are right-brain activities. It's easy to stop yourself from creatively writing because a deep desire within pharmacists is to edit, to correct a misspelled word, or to make an idea clearer. But doing so stops the creative process. Editing is the opposite of creating. So this exercise is meant to engage your right brain and lead you to your curiosity. Next I had Pooja write down these questions to ponder:

What about work seems like play at times? Have you ever felt that way?

I encouraged Pooja to focus on explaining her feelings about work, and to not feel the need to clarify, but continue writing.

In our next coaching session, Pooja said, "At first, I didn't think this exercise would help me. But I accepted the process and began to write. What I found was amazing." Pooja described her interest in hormonal therapy, specifically infertility issues. She discovered her empathy and compassion for women suffering from infertility. And she observed that she spent extra time with infertility patients in her pharmacy, even when it meant she would be behind her priorities. Pooja had rediscovered her curiosity. Months later, she was offered a job at an infertility clinic, focusing on compounding and patient counseling. Now she wakes up excited for work.

Set aside this book, download our PDF guide (*www.indispensablepharmacist.com*), and take time to rediscover your curiosity. Your future self will thank you later.

Curiosity Isn't Work; It's Play

"At the end of the day, I'm exhausted but so satisfied with the work I'm accomplishing. Time flies by. The problem I run to at work is not distinguishing priorities because I have so many projects I enjoy." That's what Leah told me about her job. She enjoys her work, the projects are challenging, and she loves the daily grind of learning and creating. It was Leah's curiosity that led her to this new role as a clinical coordinator. As an unhappy retail pharmacist, Leah had doubted whether the pharmacy profession was the right fit—then she followed her curiosity. She regularly volunteered for her company's events and did such good work that her manager easily spotted a clinical coordinator in the making (without a residency, by the way). It wasn't long before her manager began to groom Leah for the job. The transition was organic and, best of all, easy. Leah's new job is such a natural fit that it doesn't feel like "work" at all; it feels like play.

Play and work are concepts distinctly separate from each other. From a young age, you were taught that work and play didn't mix well, a distinction that became more and more pronounced as time passed. Recess gets phased out as kids get older. College professors recommend three hours of study for every credit hour of class—meaning a normal credit load of 15 hours would involved 45 additional hours of studying—a 60-hour work week. Grad students often juggle a full-time job with a full-time course load. There is no time for play, and the idea that work doesn't have to feel like drudgery sounds far-fetched. But is that true? No!

A pharmacist named Trevor had been researching functional medicine (FM) for months. Functional medicine is focused on optimal functioning of the body and usually involves holistic or alternative medicine. Trevor enjoyed the benefits of FM and, as he learned more about it, shared his knowledge with his friends. Helping others fueled his passion to begin his own FM practice. "I guess it never occurred to me that what I was doing was work," Trevor shared in a coaching session. "I love creating plans with people to help them maximize their health. This work brings so much joy and love into my life that I don't think I can do anything else."

Joy and love, two emotions everyone seeks—and few find them in their work. But for those who do, like Leah and Trevor, joy and love have made all the difference. This is why you may hear inspirational speakers say something like, "Your Monday should hold the same excitement for you as the weekend." I agree with that sentiment because waiting for the weekend day in, day out for the next 30 to 40 years of your life is no way to grow a valuable career. It creates a life in which you are never satisfied in the moment; you're either counting the hours to Friday or dreading Monday. Life becomes a series of unfortunate events with a few moments of satisfaction in between. So, since not working isn't an option for most of us, **how can you make work feel more like play**? The answer is simpler than you might think.

Pay attention to when you smile—really smile—at work. There could be a hidden gem tucked in there, and it might hold the key to changing your mindset. Maybe you haven't seen it because you put all your focus on the parts of your job that make you miserable. Choose to see the joy in your job, and you will find it. Besides, the best place to start your indispensable career is in your current job. If you can't create value in your current job, then it will be difficult to convince your next employer that you'll change.

I was in a coaching session with Katie, a pharmacist in Utah who was miserable. Her boss "hated her guts," her team was deplorable, and her stress had begun to affect her family. It was truly an awful situation.

"How long have you felt this way?" I asked her.

Katie thought for a moment. "About five years."

Imagine smoking every day for five years and then deciding that you wanted to stop. It wouldn't happen overnight, would it? There's no easy way to break entrenched habits, and shifting away from long-held negative thought patterns is not easy. Katie had been telling herself the same negative thoughts for five years and believed them wholeheartedly. Her thoughts had become her reality. She didn't see a way out of her situation because her thoughts told her there wasn't one. I began asking Katie a series of questions to find out if she was willing to change or if she wanted to stay miserable: "Are you willing to change your situation, even if it may be difficult?"

She was willing, but the change scared her.

"Are you willing to expand your love, joy, and abundance?" This question made Katie pause. "What do you mean?" she asked.

I explained that people often make excuses to justify their inaction. "There are no jobs." "No one is willing to take a chance on me." "Other people are more qualified." "I don't have enough experience." "Well," Katie admitted, "some of those do sound familiar…"

Before I could help Katie create a new strategy, I needed to know if she was willing to change her mind. Do a 180. Play with her career. Go from believing "I am miserable at work" to believing "I can experience love, joy, and abundance in any setting."

Katie was skeptical but confessed that, yes, she wanted to change and accept more love in her life, "even though it sounds kind of weird to say it out loud like that." I countered by asking her when she smiles at work. We found three areas in her current (previously described as miserable) job that involved a significant amount of play for her. Her negative perspective had blinded her to this fun side of her job. Your job has fun parts, too. The question is whether you can see them. Can you find moments of play in your workday? What about opportunities to flex your strengths? Start with these simple elements: **curiosity, joy, and play**. You don't need to find your passion; you just need to find what interests you.

Pursue Your Interests and Opportunities

"Follow your passion." "Do only work you love and the money will come." You've probably read something like these statements before. These platitudes get spread via books, inspirational Instagram feeds, and advice columns. I believed them for a long time, but then I realized the truth:

passion isn't followable. It shows up alongside you while you're doing other things.

In *So Good They Can't Ignore You*, Cal Newport shares research that shows following your passion is lousy career advice. Why? Passion changes over time. Your passions are not the same as they were when you were a child. The younger me would think I'm a weirdo for reading Japanese comics, learning magic tricks, and reading self-development books. He'd be flabbergasted to learn that my passion for comedy, Legos, and WWE didn't make it past my freshman year of college.

You've changed, too. Your passions have changed.

Seth DePasquale is a pharmacist who started his pharmacy career in retail. He didn't love it, but didn't hate it, either. He moved to a hospital setting, and felt about the same: he didn't hate it, though he DID hate the one-hour commute. Feeling the pressure to be more available to his wife and son, Seth looked for a new job closer to home. He found a part-time compounding position for a horse pharmacy. Never in his life did he think about horses or compounding, but much to Seth's surprise, he loved the work. Now, Seth is crazy passionate about compounding pharmacy, so much so that he created his own website and consulting company. Seth's passion for the subject drove him to build something more significant, but this passion was non-existent years ago—and he would never have discovered it if he were busy "following his passion" first.

Seth and I talked about it on his podcast, Pharmacy Inspection, and he reflected on a question I asked him: "What do you wish you could tell the younger you about your career?"

Seth admonished his younger self and said, "Figure your career out!" He encouraged him not to be lazy and stay complacent in his job. He shared how much happier he would be if he would have only been willing to try different things earlier. Passion is real, but using it as your sole compass may keep you from finding something better.

Now, I want to be clear: **passion is a good thing**. But there's more to your "dream job" equation than following your passion.

Newport shares in *So Good They Can't Ignore You* that if Steve Jobs were to follow his passion in his twenties, he likely would have ended up as a Zen instructor instead of the founder of one of the biggest companies in the world. Jobs didn't love computers, programming, marketing, or business; those were just quick ways to make a buck so he could go do other things. So while I agree with Newport that Jobs surely developed a passion for computers along the way, Apple started because Jobs jumped on an opportunity that fell at his feet. Following his passion had nothing to do with it. In fact, had Steve Jobs followed his actual passions, our tech landscape would probably look very different. And while that story is about a larger-than-life innovator, its implications for PharmDs (and anyone else, for that matter) hold true.

Seth DePasquale discovered his passion for compounding pharmacy because he was looking for a shorter commute. Once he realized how much he enjoyed his new job, he pursued it with hustle. He's growing his passion every day by practicing it in his job and hustling at night (or early mornings) to create additional opportunities to do what he loves.

And that brings us to another critical element: pursuit.

What led Seth to his passion was the skill of pursuit. He did the work of educating himself about compounding pharmacy, he practiced, he explored new ideas and figured out what other people were doing, developing, and innovating. Seth pursued his interests and opportunities into every corner they led him. Pushing oneself to try new things, even risky things, is how passion develops. Passion isn't this part of you that was always there. Those are gifts, natural talents, strengths, or whatever you'd like to call them. You may find you enjoy practicing your strength, but passion comes after you've discovered your unique ability and a desire to grow it.

YOUR UNIQUE ABILITY AND ZONE OF GENIUS

"What's your special power?" I asked my six-year-old daughter, Izzie, one weeknight. She thought it over for a moment and replied, "My superpower is being nice," and then proceeded to tell me about this new Pokémon™ toy she wants. She's spot on. Izzie is a team player. In her class, she makes others feel welcome. She isn't one to hog the spotlight. Instead, she encourages others do their best. Everyone has a unique ability, an inherent strength or skill that influences your ability to do a job well. Developing your ability into an expertise moves it into your "zone of genius," a concept discussed at length in Gay Hendricks's book, The Big Leap, and Dan Sullivan's Pure Genius. Being in your zone of genius elicits inner feelings like, "This is what I was born to do!" It feels great, and those who play in their zone of genius typically become shining examples of happy career people. But I argue that it's not enough to just identify and participate in your zone of genius; you have to take it a step further and put it to work in a purposeful way. Unfortunately, many pharmacists spend work in areas outside their zone of genius, where they have either minimal natural ability or outright hate doing something. Whether it's because they're spinning their wheels or because their employer requires it, PharmDs burn a lot of time in their "zone of competence."

The Zone of Competence

The word "competence" in healthcare carries a challenging connotation. Typically, when "competence" comes up, the conversation is about how someone wasn't "smart enough" to do a job. Every single pharmacist has a degree declaring him or her competent in areas of pharmacy practice, so in our world, "competent" is just a shade above "has a pulse." Competence is the minimum standard, the lowest expectation. The zone of competence describes work you find boring and time-wasting. It encompasses the wide range of activities you can execute successfully. You may not enjoy all of them (in fact, you may loathe some), but you can do them without burning the building down. This zone is where thousands of pharmacists find themselves day in, day out. Staying in this zone creates boredom, unfulfillment, and eventually burnout if stress is present. Most pharmacists are competent in their role. But the simply competent pharmacist is unlikely to find satisfaction or do her best work.

The Zone of Excellence

You are excellent at a few things, but the list is smaller than your zone of competence. You can be trusted to do these things well. You know that others hear how good you are in this area—maybe they're even a little jealous. In fact, you may not like being in your zone of excellence all the time because it may feel like others can't catch up to you. It's comfortable to stay here, but you'll eventually say to yourself, "I feel like I'm not giving my best." Great things happen when you push even further, into your zone of genius.

The Zone of Genius

Your zone of genius is the place where your work makes you feel alive, like you're doing the most good in the world. Your unique ability and interests align. Your work feels purposeful and fulfilling. Rineil was a practicing retail pharmacist for five years in the Los Angeles market, hated his job, and felt trapped in the community setting. That's why he reached out to me. One coaching session in particular stands out.

We were discussing his past interests and how Rineil chose to spend his spare time. Rineil loved cars. He would buy cheap junkers and build them up over time. He "traded up" materials to make the original car perform better. Then, once he felt finished the project, he would sell the car for a hefty profit. It didn't feel like work, he shared with me. He found the process enjoyable, almost like a game. When he said the word "process," I knew we stumbled across something big. He shared that his whole life had been about hacking processes, even at his day job. The thing that makes him stand out at work, he told me, was how great he was at systems management and process improvement. Of course, he was too humble to use the word "great," but it was clear we had uncovered Rineil's unique ability—his zone of genius. Rineil ultimately decided that his unique ability would be put to better use outside of pharmacy, so he started his own business. He loves his work within his zone of genius and gets to flex his unique ability every day. If you'd like to read more about Rineil's progress, check out his blog on *TheHappyPharmD.com*. Oh, and I should mention he moved out of community pharmacy quickly and into a low-stress outpatient clinic within five months after we started working together. That's really fast timing considering the average job hunt takes nine months. Just like Rineil, you have a unique ability that, when practiced, enters you into your zone of genius. Everyone has some talent or natural ability that they do well. But how do you find it?

What Is Your Unique Ability?

Your unique ability should inspire you to move deeper into your work. Maybe your job holds activities that play into your zone of genius. Perhaps there's a problem at work no one is willing to touch—could it be an opportunity for you to flex your unique ability?

Don't be disappointed in yourself if, like Rineil, you find your genius outside of the pharmacy profession. I remember my sinking feeling when I realized that I loved teaching but didn't want to be a full-time professor. If your zone of genius is playing guitar, then pharmacy may not be an avenue that values your ability. But don't let that stop you from experimenting! You could be the next pharmacist/musician to educate patients through the power of song.

Let's ask some questions to dive deeper into your unique ability.

What work do you most enjoy?

Zach was a pharmacist in the typical retail setting: overworked, overstressed, and underdeveloped by management. He came to me wondering, "How can I find something more fulfilling?"

In a coaching session, I asked Zach multiple questions about what he found fulfilling like, "What work do you most enjoy?" What I've discovered from pharmacists in almost every dead-end job setting is that they can find something about their work that brings them a sliver of satisfaction. Zach shared a few things that he enjoyed, such as patient health screenings, immunizations, and administration system-oriented tasks. With a little more digging and a few phone calls, Zach now regularly runs health-screening events not just at his store, but at stores all across his state, taking him away from boring tasks.

Uncovering the work that brings you joy is the first step to discovering your zone of genius. However, this question is more like a shotgun approach. The second question is like a sniper rifle.

What brings you the most satisfaction at work?

Another way to ask this question is this, "What work brings the highest ratio of fulfillment to time spent?" You may spend only a few minutes doing the work, but it makes the whole day seem brighter. After we discovered Macie's unique ability for writing and editing, she shared this about her "work" after practicing it for three months:

"My mood all day today has been affected by my writing in the morning." When I pried for more information, she said, "I spent just twenty minutes writing an article for a website, and I felt alive in the process. Like none of my worries mattered anymore. They all came back to me when I finished writing, but during those moments I felt joyful the rest of the day."

Twenty minutes of satisfying work turned her whole day around.

If no ideas spring forward from your work or past jobs, then it's time to consider other areas of life, like hobbies or entertainment. I recently met a teacher who quit his job years ago to become an online Dungeons and Dragons expert. He consults people who play the game and makes YouTube videos. There is no limitation on what you can do with your unique ability. Once you enter the zone of genius, opportunities (in any area of life) begin presenting themselves.

What about this work makes it so satisfying?

When I'm with a small group of pharmacists and I ask this powerful question, the emotional response always takes me aback. The way people describe why their work is satisfying holds a deep connection with a person and others. For a quick example of this, just watch any video of Elon Musk talking about rockets to Mars. The guy would probably marry a rocket if he could.

Your answer to this third question may be your best clue to your unique ability. If you struggle to explain why the work is satisfying, you may have found your genius. Happy work is difficult to describe because it connects with a deep emotional part of you that you may not have the vocabulary to express. I believe nearly all people struggle with communicating what they are amazing at simply because they haven't been given the tools or practice to do so. Nonetheless, I encourage you to try.

Write down your answers to put your genius into words. Describe your feelings when you do the work. What do you feel like after the experience? Ask close friends or family members to confirm your thoughts. Do they see this experience in you? Can they confirm this to be your unique ability? It may surprise you to learn how readily apparent your unique ability is to those who know you best.

What Stops People from Entering Their Zone of Genius?

If stepping into your zone of genius is so easy, then why doesn't everyone do their best work? Well, being genius doesn't come without its pressures. A close friend of mine often quotes a New York Times article when talking about why people don't do what they say they're going to do. "Eighty-one percent of Americans feel they have a book in them—and that they should write it."

The point being that people, even humble ones, want to achieve greatness, but rarely do they follow through. I encourage you to be one of the 1% that finishes. I have yet to hear a client say he regrets pursuing his unique ability.

Your unique ability will be the foundation of your indispensable career. Hopefully by now you have an idea of what your ability might be. (If not, there are a few resources I recommend you use on our website **[INSERT WEBSITE]**). You may be asking, "Now what? How can I possibly use my unique ability in a career?"

You'll use your zone of genius to dream up ideas, create new projects, connect with influencers, and eventually land a new job or start a business or a freelancer role. First, we should consider your unique ability and how it fits into the marketplace. Many people think the easiest way to get a new job is by scanning through job boards. Not so. Even less-than-desirable jobs (I'm talking floater jobs at bad chain stores) receive over 100 applications. By sticking to the obvious targets, you set yourself up to compete with plenty of candidates who may have more experience or better connections than you. Why would you compete with everyone for the worst opportunities? The way to find a job that fits your unique skills is by creating the opportunity yourself. Note: I don't mean that you are creating a job. You are creating the opportunity to meet someone, to hear about an opening that isn't listed on a job board, or create a potential side job.

In order to discover how your genius fits into the marketplace, let's talk about your ikigai.

YOUR IKIGAI

When I met Tracy, I knew things were tough. She worked in community pharmacy for a little over a decade but had recently been let go from a major retailer on a mission to cut staff. She took a similar position at a smaller chain store, but it wasn't going well. Tracy was unhappy and questioning whether she ought to leave pharmacy altogether. On one of our calls, I introduced to her the Japanese concept of *ikigai*, which at its simplest could be described as a reason for being—but it goes way beyond that. Ikigai is infused with purpose, dedication, craftsmanship, joy, and contribution.

Tracy's career met three out of the four cornerstones of ikigai:

- What the world needs: The world needs pharmacists. What others will pay you to do: Companies are willing to pay for pharmacists.

- What you're good at: Tracy was good at her job; she's no slouch. As for the fourth—what you love— well... that one was missing. After a few conversations, we discovered something unique about Tracy: her passion for preparedness. Ask her to open her car trunk and you'll find a pack of emergency tools, flashlight, blanket, and a few MREs (meals ready to eat). Ever since she was a child, her father had pushed into her head the importance of being ready for anything, and it paid off. Tracy had been the responsible one throughout school and had saved her friends on more than one occasion. Maybe we could find an intersection between this love and her work.

It didn't take long. Tracy found a job opening in a state government agency that needed an "emergency preparedness" pharmacist. Suddenly, it was like someone had lit a fire under Tracy's butt. She wanted that job! Tracy's passion fueled her vigor to build a relationship with the manager before and after the interview. She found a local conference about emergency preparedness. She started to ask more questions about emergency preparedness with facility managers and directors and practiced her communication skills before the interview so they knew she cared about this job and wasn't just another burned-out pharmacist who hated her work. It's amazing to see what can happen when things snap into alignment. Tracy's new job matched her ikigai perfectly:

- What the world needs: The world needs to be prepared for disasters!

- What others will pay you to do: Government agencies will pay for specialists

- What she's good at: Systems management and improvement

- What she loves: Emergency preparedness

After receiving the offer from the government agency, Tracy shared, "I'm not used to things going well for me!" *What's Your Ikigai?*

Many of my clients feel like work is just a means to an end. They get paid, but the money isn't fulfilling. Life becomes full of stuff they need to pay down continually. They show up to work every day and go through the motions. Punch in, punch out, repeat. They feel comfortable but empty. Or they may say they feel useless, as though their work means nothing.

But something amazing happens when your work becomes a part of your reason for being. The Japanese call this concept *ikigai* (pronounced "ee-kee-guy"). Ikigai work should combine the following:

- What you're good at

- What the world needs

- What others will pay you to do

- What you love

Most pharmacists do things that fall into two categories: What the world needs (pharmacists) and what you can get paid for (by having a degree that qualifies you for the job). But if those pharmacists hate their work, then pharmacy is not their ikigai. Skill isn't enough to create fulfilling work. I'm great at shuffling cards, but I don't want to be a dealer in Vegas. Love alone won't cut it either, I'm afraid. If no one is willing to pay you for your pig Latin translation class, then you'll need to keep that as a hobby and not a career. The point is to strike a balance between *what you like to do*, *what you're good at*, and *what the world needs* enough to *pay you to provide*. As we're about to see, your zone of genius and *ikigai* can take you to some unexpected places.

Start with Your Unique Ability

During my fourth year of pharmacy school, I was in panic mode for months. I realized that I wanted to commit myself to the residency path but, unfortunately, I had done nothing to make me a strong candidate.

My panic forced me into a corner. I needed something to boost my CV and make myself a stronger candidate for residency, so my eye turned to teaching, my unique ability. Lectures were the quickest thing I could manage during my rotations. I found it easy, plus lots of people wanted my skill. I volunteered to teach mid-level practitioners, nursing students, PA students, pharmacy students, and patients. The lectures fell squarely in my zone of genius. I felt like I was on fire with passion. Even if the subject was boring to me, like heart failure medications, I taught it with excitement. My creativity poured out because I wanted to do a great job teaching the materials. I remember one lecture in particular about OTC skin care. I knew the subject bored the class, so I created a skit for two students to act out. One played a pharmacist, and another student played an adolescent boy who had a crush on her. The pharmacist brushed aside his flirtations and tried to educate him on acne medications. It was a riot, and the students loved it. I remember watching them, thinking, "This is what I need to do all the time." Even as I write this short story, I find myself overcome with joy by the experience.

More opportunities presented themselves to me as I taught more and more. People would approach me with opportunities to speak at meet-ups, schools, and patient groups. I learned of lecture opportunities at colleges and even was approached to apply to two faculty positions once I finished my residency. These things happen when you operate in your zone of genius. Others see the genius within you and want to help you operate further in this zone. You'll find more opportunities to operate in your zone of genius as you practice your unique ability. The indispensable pharmacist eventually has to turn down these opportunities because there are too many. The first step is getting started.

Are you ready to help others with your unique ability?

Volunteer Your Ability

Find a need in your community, an event coming up, or an organization you believe in. Sometimes it just takes getting off your butt. My friend Chris wondered how he could get started working in his zone of genius more often. He is passionate about rescuing animals, so I challenged him to help a local animal hospital. Just the act of volunteering motivated him to ask himself a new question: "Where can I best place my energy and passion?" His energies focused on a new path, which led him to receive more job offers than he can handle. So, where can you put your unique ability to work?

Find a weakness. After the six-month mark at a job, most of us can pinpoint our workplace's weak spots. Within the first two months of starting my job, I found inefficiencies in the workflow. I wished to share my discoveries on becoming more efficient with others. Unfortunately, my coworkers didn't see the issues I did and didn't want to fix them. So my unique ability (teaching) wasn't activated. Their disinterest stripped me of the motivation to pursue other opportunities to express my unique ability at work. Luckily, I found an opportunity to do so outside of work. I volunteered to teach a class at a clinic, and my help was gladly accepted.

Weaknesses at work are everywhere, and you can help fill those with your unique ability. If you can't find something, then talk to your manager. Find out his priorities and learn how you could fit into solving those problems.

A caution to those who are under-performing: Don't approach your manager from a position of weakness. Josh, a student of mine in Career Jumpstart, found a roadblock in expressing his unique ability in information technology. He wanted to learn more about how he could do more work in IT and approached his manager to ask for advice. His manager pointed out that Josh wasn't doing well with his current metrics and expressed concern that working on other projects would further diminish his performance. Josh came back with, "But no one else is performing to the standard metrics..." and his manager let him have it. She described several pharmacists who were meeting their goals and how they were doing it. It was a hard lesson for Josh, but it set him on a different path. He spoke with other top-performing pharmacists and found out how to improve. Now that Josh has improved his performance, he has been speaking with the IT department in both his full-time and part-time jobs and has gained confidence through experience.

If your performance is in question, then it will be difficult to get your manager on board with any new changes you recommend. Find a path forward to improve your current job so the opportunities flow your way.

Reach out to your association. Associations are always looking for help. Call your state group and find out if you can volunteer your unique ability. Lauren recently launched her ability into the stratosphere. She has a passion for functional medicine, the medical practice that focuses on optimal functioning of the body. Her unique ability is organization and leadership. She started an organization within pharmacy to promote awareness and has been spreading the good news from association to association, expressing her unique ability along the way. Now opportunities keep opening for her everywhere she goes, particularly speaking engagements and leading her organization!

Don't be disappointed. Many pharmacists find a new passion within themselves to express their unique ability. At some point, you will run into a roadblock. The opportunities presented to you won't be perfect. You might not be expressing yourself in the opportunity. It may not be a perfect fit. And that's okay. In the beginning, it's best to express your ability with any short-term commitment. You'll discover things you like (and dislike), which will help you refine your search for greater opportunities. Your ability is like an onion. You can pull back layers of your ability to find what you love to do as you practice it.

Solve Problems

Every job exists to solve a problem, and given that the world has so many, you have unlimited opportunity to find an issue challenging, fulfilling, and engaging enough to make you want to attempt a solution. What problem do you want to solve? I've noticed a wave of new practitioners who have become disenchanted with the community pharmacy setting of healthcare. Many pharmacists tell me they believe the American public is overmedicated and wish their jobs could focus on preventive health. My friend Lauren Castle felt the same way. She saw a huge problem in our healthcare system: functional medicine doesn't have a presence in pharmacy. That's why she started the Functional Medicine Pharmacist Association.

The problem doesn't have to be in pharmacy. The problem can be about world hunger or a lack of Thai restaurants in your area (my personal problem... please, someone come to where I live and start a Thai restaurant) or poor posture. Imagine a pharmacist who became obsessed with helping other pharmacists with their posture problems. This pharmacist could talk to an OT colleague, a designer friend, and a manufacturer in China. After enough research and talking with people, this pharmacist could create a shoe or floor mat or hidden posture enhancer to help pharmacists across the world stand at ease and without pain. Problems exist everywhere. **Is there a certain problem you keep returning to?** Did you know that we landed on the moon before we put wheels on luggage? You don't have to come up with some out-of-this-world innovation; you just have to keep an eye out for complaints and inconveniences. A client of mine, Collin, decided to start a consulting business specializing in performing prior authorizations after he kept hearing of physician offices complaining about prior authorizations. In many ways, he found his *ikigai* just by listening to others. Create a list of problems that occur to you on a daily basis. Highlight the ones that interest you. Look for a solution or find the available solutions and critique them. Could you build a better widget?

What frustrates you? If I'm honest, the problem of unhappy pharmacists really frustrates me. I hated feeling like I was in a career prison. I hate it even more when other people feel trapped. This was a major motivator for creating *The Happy PharmD* and this book. Surely there is a problem at work that makes you mad. Rather than complain, could you try to solve it? Could you attempt to move past (mental) barriers like "We've tried to fix it," or, "No one listens to my ideas," or, "It's because of so-and-so that we can't resolve this issue."?

What if you became the go-to person who fixes a certain problem? By becoming an expert in QS1™ (a prescription management and process system) while working as a community pharmacist, an anonymous pharmacist told me he was able to build relationships with QS1 while working to improve the software. He loved the program and enjoyed "hacking" the system to improve his workflow. Other pharmacists would always field questions to him because he built a reputation as the "go-to QS1 guy." QS1 enjoyed his passion and involvement so much so that they poached him from his job. He now works with QS1 as a trainer and company liaison. The "go-to" person implies indispensable value. Your company has so many problems to solve that people are assigned to tasks to solve them. What roles or responsibilities could you volunteer for to highlight your unique ability?

What kinds of problems are you always solving? You have a reputation at work, whether by design or not. People know you by your distinguishable characteristics. Perhaps you are the go-to for a certain problem. The problems you fix should align with your unique ability. I'll never start a business involving mechanical problems. Why? Because I suck at fixing anything physical. I'm not mechanically gifted. If you were to ask me to start a business that focuses on solving those kinds of issues, I wouldn't last long. I would become frustrated and quit, or would have to issue so many refunds that the business would be untenable. You may notice you tend to avoid particular tasks and involve yourself in certain issues. Pay attention to the ones you keep returning to. It could be a sign that you enjoy that kind of work.

Review your work history. Have you noticed any trends of problems you're always solving? What solved problems have you found consistently create fulfillment?

What problems can you solve for someone else? Every company has problems. You'll find them mentioned in email newsletters, company meetings, and complaints from your colleagues. Your ability to solve other people's problems could lead to a promotion or being hired by another company.

Collin was a new grad in a bad market. He joined retail pharmacy after graduation and felt like most retail pharmacists: "I can't do this forever." Collin started a winding road from consulting to entrepreneurship, but he finally landed an exciting job at a startup company called Roman, a men's health (specifically erectile dysfunction) prescribing and delivery business. What's interesting about his story is how he solved a problem for the startup before he was offered a position. He began an email conversation with the founder (who he found on Craigslist) and, after conversing back and forth, Collin decided to take a small "risk." He created an erectile dysfunction drug class market analysis for the founder. Collin told me over the phone, "I thought it would be really valuable to him. But I didn't think much of it because I didn't picture myself in the position. I wasn't even thinking, 'Maybe he'll hire me.'" This analysis was exactly the kind of work the founder was looking for and immediately emailed Collin back with the simple message: "We need to meet in person." Collin accepted his job offer shortly thereafter.

You could also be the one who leads the charge to solve problems and create your own opportunities. Donald worked at a call-center pharmacy. He thought his job was okay, but nothing inspiring. He wondered whether he could transition to a different career path and what it might be, so Donald attended my biannual event, The Happy PharmD Summit. He listened to pharmacists in the information technology space. He thought it would be very interesting.

After joining our Career Jumpstart, a class that teaches pharmacists how to transition into a new career, Donald learned how he could start his journey into IT pharmacy immediately. Rather than focusing on a degree (which does not guarantee a job, as we pharmacists have learned), Donald created opportunities for himself. He started by conversing with IT Pharmacists. He learned their perspectives, the problems they work on, and began to think differently at his previously despised job. Then he reached out to the IT department and invited the manager to lunch. They talked over BBQ brisket and brainstormed new ways for them to develop their software. He has gained IT experience by volunteering for projects and is hustling his way into work he finds more fulfilling.

What does the world need? The pharmacy world has a plethora of problems. Whether you want to focus on our broken health care system, or third-world issues, or even first-world problems (why can't I receive pad Thai by drone yet?), there's no end to your options. The world needs and is willing to pay for solutions. Carlos, a full-time community pharmacist, and his wife found a problem with Uber. While Uber is a safe and reliable option for transportation, it has a strict policy against driving unaccompanied minors. You can imagine busy parents would have the need to transport children when they aren't available. Carlos and his wife created the startup Care Commute, which offers transportation just for minors. It's like a shuttle bus program you can trust. Carlos found a problem and created a solution, and the company has done well enough to allow Carlos' wife to work full-time on the business. But you don't need to start up a company to solve a problem. Your current employer has plenty of issues to overcome. Hopefully one of their problems is interesting to you. If you have an idea of where you want your career to go, you can attempt to solve the problem in hopes this will bolster your resume for the next job. For example, an academic or MSL job manager will be more interested in you as a candidate if you have teaching experience. Volunteer yourself to teach patients, students, or medical professionals. What could be a better way to be seen as an expert than by teaching others?

What change do you want to see in the world? My father left my mom and me when I was two years old. He began an affair with another woman shortly after I was conceived and was living two separate lives for a while. My mom attempted to save the marriage, but he decided to not be a part of our lives. For a long time I believed my father leaving didn't affect me. I was too young to understand or perceive the situation. It wasn't until I graduated college that I truly understood how this affected my whole life and made me who I am today. I believe without the influence and love of my father, I became a child of constant envy for attention. I was the perpetual class clown. I even earned the title in my graduation yearbook. I can't imagine what my life would be like if my "dad" didn't step into my life when I was five. I call Mike Barker my dad because he took me in as his own son. He treated me like a real father should treat a son. I'm forever grateful for his sacrifices, teachings, and leadership (by example). When I was 12, I legally changed my last name to Barker, hence why I'm not "Alex Richie" anymore. My dad, in a way, adopted me. He saved me from a life of pain and showed me by example what it means to be a man. I wouldn't be writing this book if it weren't for him. Because of my dad, I became passionate about adoption. Adoption holds the power to forever change a person's life. Not just the child who's adopted, but parents, extended family, community, future friends, and the list goes on. One adoption creates a ripple effect of change. The change I want to see in this world is more families adopting unwanted kids. The problem is adoption prices are ridiculously high. I called an adoption center and found the price of an American adoption is about $25,000. To adopt a child outside the country is $35,000, minimum. Most Americans live paycheck to paycheck. There's almost no way a family could afford to adopt. My solution: raise and donate $25,000 per year from my business to help one family adopt a child. Truthfully, I don't know how I'm going to accomplish this yet, but I have a feeling I can achieve it. I'm starting this process by donating 10% of profits from this book to my yearly adoption fund. What change in the world do you desire? You don't have to be a pharmacist to make a big impact on the world or find fulfillment in work. Most famous people are not pharmacists. #funfact. You have something in your life you care about deeply. It doesn't have to be career-related. You could care about the starving people in North Korea, or the civil war in Yemen, or the homeless people in your community. The change will only happen if you attempt to solve it. Here are a few questions to get you going toward solving problems:

- What problems in the world do you want to solve?

- What problems do you struggle with on a daily basis?

- How could you attempt to create a solution? Could you create a product or a solution to your problem? Do you know others with the same problem as you? Could you help others fix the same problem you faced?

- What interests have you held over the years?

And finally, **what problems will someone else pay you to solve?**

Get Paid

Imagine explaining the internet to someone from the 1980s. Odds are you'd be met with a blank stare. If you're looking for a problem to solve that results in a job offer, I encourage you to look to the future. Every profession advances, and pharmacy is no exception. I believe pharmacist responsibilities (like verification) will either be automated by machines or handed to technicians. You won't do your career any favors by becoming an expert at verifying prescriptions. Looking ahead to the future's problems ensures a secure career or business. Finding the future's problems creates a unique position for yourself, as you become (ideally) the go-to person to solve them.

I recently had the pleasure of listening to a panel of experts in the pharmacy field. One panelist was quite the accomplished pharmacist. He shared how he was responsible for helping a few major retail pharmacy chains go digital from analog in the 1980s and 1990s. Rest assured, he was well-compensated for this work and continued to receive job opportunities well after his work in the '80s.

If our profession's problems don't interest you, then have no worries. There are plenty of problems companies are willing to pay employees to solve. Your task is to match companies' needs (if you want to be employed) or the needs of customers (if you want to start a business) with your zone of genius.

What the world needs + what you can get paid to do + what you're good at + what you love... the four elements of your *ikigai* are simple on their own—but, of course, finding your *ikigai* won't necessarily happen overnight. Don't let that dissuade you! If you can find a way to draw even one of those elements into your work life, you may be surprised by its impact. Better still, if you find a way to create impact, you may find your work feels much more meaningful.

Create Impact

No pharmacy student graduates with the thought, "I can't wait to make [insert chain pharmacy name here] more money!" Pharmacists are desperate for a job that provides meaning, not be harped on to meet metrics so the shareholders can be happy. A job without meaning makes you feel like a cog in a machine. You have one chance to live your life. I encourage you to work at a job that creates meaning. When you have a job that creates a sense of purpose and significance, you'll notice subtle changes. First, your curiosity wakes up. Amy, a retail pharmacist who transitioned into a regulatory affairs position, told me, "Just the change in environment made me feel comfortable to pursue ideas and projects I had no knowledge in. I felt safe."

With purpose, work becomes a place of play—but with meaning. When I play a game of Settlers of Catan™ with friends, I view it as a superfluous but good time. When I play Old Maid™ with my daughters, I see it as a time for building deep connections with my children and a chance to teach them how to handle disappointment. Your work can become a place for you to explore your curiosity and fulfill the needs of the company. Can you see the difference between play and play with meaning?

The easiest way to make your work matter now is to infuse it with meaning *now*. What steps can you take today to ensure you feel proud of the life you live and the work you do?

ONE LIFE

You have one life to accomplish what you desire. You should never expect your perfect job to just come to you.

I once spoke with a pharmacist, Rachel, who saw roadblocks everywhere she looked. She hated her monotonous job and knew she was ready for a transition—we were off to a great start—but as I asked her questions about her potential interests, Rachel quickly followed each answer with why she couldn't pursue them. For example, she was interested in academia, but she wanted to avoid the politics (I can relate to her on that one). She wouldn't stop bringing up roadblocks to different career paths. I eventually asked her: "Do you expect your next career move to be easy?" Do you?

You have one life to live. Even if you believe in reincarnation, you don't get a do-over of this life. This life is difficult. Opportunities won't be handed to you. Failures will come. Roadblocks will unexpectedly pop up. Are you wasting your talents, or are you striving toward a great and fulfilling career? And when your time runs out and you're about to shuffle off the ol' mortal coil, dust to dust and all that, will you be satisfied with the life you lived?

The best way to plan your career move is to understand where your whole life is going. I coached enough pharmacists to understand that your next career step doesn't provide adequate guidance to make a great next step in the right direction. So, how do you know your next career leap will take you in the direction you want?

Begin with the End in Mind

This exercise may be scary for some, but, trust me: contemplating your own death can shine a bright light on the way you're living now. My advice? Dive into the work and don't try to fight the emotions that bubble up—because bubble up they will.

Imagine you are watching your own funeral. You can smell the flowers and hear the murmurings of your assembled loved ones.

Who is there?

What are they saying about you?

The answers to these questions will summarize the impact of your life. When you die, you will leave behind a legacy created by your everyday decisions—like the decision to say a kind word or to sacrifice a weekend for a friend. Or the decision to put in overtime (again) at work instead of leaving early to catch your daughter's recital. Or choosing to deny yourself something you want or need. "I regret not doing..."

Maybe you feel like you have unfinished business to attend to. Maybe you need to apologize to a friend or forgive another. Maybe you need to buy that plane ticket or take that dream vacation. Perhaps you need to speak up for yourself. It's the clarity that comes from this bird's-eye view that makes this exercise so effective. As Candy Chang put it, "Thinking about death clarifies your life." So let's take this exercise a little deeper.

Write your eulogy. Imagine who is attending your memorial and what they'll say about you. Some of your eulogy may describe how you are now or how you aspire to be. What makes this exercise so impactful is what I call your "eulogy gaps." The things that impacted me most—and made me blubber like a baby—were the areas where I could see a clear gap (or in some cases, a crevasse) between what I hoped people would say and what I *knew* they would say. Those were the spots where I realized I was falling short. When I first went through this exercise, I remember writing my oldest daughter saying, "Alex was the best father there ever was." I nearly cried after finishing the sentence (a rarity for me, unless I'm watching *The Notebook* or the end of the *Lord of the Rings* movies... I know I'm different). I realized I wasn't living up to my potential as a father, and it immediately motivated me to makes some changes to become better for my girls. It was hard to see that disparity so clearly, and my gaps showed me where I needed to make a change. Gaps in your family, health, and work may become apparent as you describe what is said in your eulogy. You may find a large gap in your career. This is good. It's the first step toward change.

The next step, listing my life accounts, helped me clarify my gaps even further.

List your life accounts. Thinking about your end will make you reflect on what is important: relationships, accomplishments, special moments—those things that truly matter to you. We can summarize these areas as life accounts. **What are the most essential things in your life?** Use simple one or two word answers, like health, work, passion, church, or family. At the end, you should have four to ten (or more) in this list. Here are my life accounts in no particular order:

- Spiritual health

- Challenges—mental and physical health

- Family—My wife, Megan, and my kids, Izzie and Addie

- Close friendships

- Vocation

- Finances

- Giving

After summarizing your life accounts, you now have a base to work with. From here, you can figure out how to close your gaps.

Look for gaps and discrepancies. I do this exercise about once a year, assessing all the things in my life, good and bad. It's a great way to illuminate the areas where I'm missing the mark. For example, after putting my kids to bed, my wife and I used to enjoy around two hours of TV shows or video games. For a while I loved the escape from daily pressures. The time spent was relaxing was wonderful. However, I felt the excessive consumption eat away at other areas of my life. I like to get up early. Five a.m. is a spectacular time to get work done (like this book). However, my late nights gaming (10:30-11:00pm) would cause me to sleep in. I would lose out on a solid two hours of hustle time. This eulogy and life accounts exercise showed me an area of my life that had grown too heavy. And so I changed my habits to change my life:

- Spend two nights every week after the kids go to bed reading a book and spending time with friends or Megan.

- Limit video games and TV shows, when used, to no later than 10:00 pm.

The idea that "what got you here won't get you there" is on full display when you're staring at the gaps in your life accounts. If writing your eulogy shows you the areas where you aren't living the way you want to, then it's time to admit that you need to change course. What activities, exercises, or habits must you implement in your career to change its trajectory? Creating your career's eulogy should show where you'd like to end up; the path may not be clear but the impact of your work will be. To close the gap between where you are now and where you want to be, something must change. What are you willing to commit to change?

A POWERFUL NEW WAY
OF LIVING

At some point in your career, you felt conflict and dis-appointment—sometimes simultaneously. You will probably experience them in the future, too. The cause doesn't really matter; disappointment and conflict can come from anywhere. What matters is why the experience impacted you the way it did. Nearly every conflict boils down to unmet expectations. You expect to be treated fairly and respectfully. You expect others to listen. But these things don't happen and the disappointment it triggers tends to come from a deep emotional place. You come home, and your husband hasn't done that chore after he said he would. Unmet expectation. Your coworker is late again, and you have to cover for her. Unmet expectation. Your technician openly disrespects you and avoids consequence. Unmet expectation. Your boss ignored your request for a necessary workflow improvement. Unmet expectation. All these unmet expectations add up, and the result is disappointment, frustration, and, if it gets to be too much, conflict.

Thousands of pharmacists get stuck in an endless cycle of failed expectations, specifically in their careers. They expect to be left to do their work peacefully and safely, yet are always distracted from their work and even disrespected by healthcare professionals and patients. Conflict is likely the reason why so many pharmacists hate what they do. How can you fix this? Is there no escape from the endless cycle of conflict?

Let me present a new way of thinking. Instead of living your life as a series of expectations, try making *agreements*.

An expectation is a strong belief that something will happen or be the case in the future. Often, expectations are not communicated, or, if they are, the other side has not been given the option to agree. The fact that everyone involved is not on the same page makes it easy for those expectations to go unmet. An agreement, on the other hand, avoids that disconnect because both parties agree to the same set of terms. Sadly, this rarely happens in life, let alone the workplace. Imagine saying to each patient, "Do you agree to treat me with respect?" I know, I know—but think of all the unpleasant patient interactions such an agreement could prevent!

So, what can you agree to right now?

Do you want to create a life full of fulfilling work?

If so, then commit yourself to keep reading.

Do you want to move away from a job that limits the fullest expression of you?

If your answer is yes, then commit yourself to taking small actions toward your goal.

Make a powerful agreement with yourself, with your spouse, with your father, mother, brother, sister, colleague, friend, or even me, the guy who you'll be hanging out with for the rest of this book.

Make an agreement with yourself that you will no longer stand to be a pharmacist who accepts job conditions as they are. You will accept circumstances that favor your best self.

Do it now. Don't worry. I'll wait right here.

I Agree to...

_____

_____

_____

_____

_____

_____

A Powerful New Mindset

Agreements are a fantastic tool for changing your mindset, and they're particularly useful when you can't do much to alter or improve your external circumstances.

The pharmacist spends her day doing work that never ends—comparable to the factory line worker, only the production line is people and medicine. When the pharmacist returns to her next shift, the work doesn't change; it's the same tasks over and over, and the only end in sight is the changing of the guard. Sound familiar?

The problem with the production line analogy is that it doesn't account for the competing priorities the pharmacist has to manage. So, let's expand on the analogy a bit more. The pharmacist has multiple lines of production to work on, each with work demanding her attention to meet impossible metrics. The painful part of each production line is that she knows if she spends too much time in one line, she won't finish her priorities in agreement with management. But the problem with trying to appease management is that they dictate priorities that consistently conflict with each other. She begins to compare herself to the machinery that assists her. She's just another mindless part of the pharmacy machine.

The pharmacist cog believes certain things to maintain her cog-like status:

- I cannot change.

- I'm stuck in this situation.

- I can't leave this job because [insert limiting belief].

- I cannot get ahead in my work.

These beliefs stop the pharmacist cog from becoming a fulfilled and happy pharmacist.

The fulfilled pharmacist believes:

- I can change.

- I can get out of any situation.

- I could leave my job at any time if I wanted to.

- I can get ahead in my work.

The fulfilled pharmacist believes other things, too, and makes the following agreements with herself:

- I will follow my interests.

- I will volunteer for things that I'm passionate about.

- My work schedule does not bind my time.

A pharmacist who doesn't change her thoughts will stay where she is or, at best, only move forward slightly. If a pharmacist believes the first set of limiting beliefs ("I cannot find a job"), why would she attempt to change her position? Humans are made to follow their beliefs. A Democrat won't vote Republican. A vegan won't eat meat. A defeated pharmacist won't change her career. Beliefs must change first, but you can't just adopt a new set of beliefs and change your life. How can you change your beliefs easily? **Take action and belief will follow**.

You Have so Much Potential in You

If you want to move into the next phase of your career, then there's a shedding you need to do. You may find that you have thoughts keeping you in your comfort zone. I call them limiting beliefs. Everyone has them, including me. Ridding yourself of them is necessary to move into work you love because these beliefs will do everything they can to keep you where you're comfortable. But the stakes are much higher than "stretching yourself" or "staying comfortable."

In nature, there is growth or death. There is no in between, and if you're not growing, you're dying. You likely have plenty of limiting beliefs disguised as excuses for your situation and why you can't change. That's your fear wanting to prevent you from failure, but trying and failing is still progress. **Doing nothing is the real failure.** I believe in you. I know you're immensely capable of creating the life you want. I mean, look at you! You completed pharmacy school. You've built out a career. You handle multiple priorities: work, family, love, hobbies, passions, interests, extracurriculars, and life goals. You've done so much already and still have so much to offer. I want to show you how to get past your limiting beliefs and grow to new heights in your career.

Let's start by creating powerful agreements. If you say "yes" to these questions, then you're ready to take the next step into work you love.

Do you want to move toward being happier?

Do you want to live fully in your zone of genius?

Do you want to work on things you love?

When I ask this question to a crowd of pharmacists, the majority answer, "yes." If I ask, "Are you currently doing what you love?" the yeses significantly decrease.

Do you want to make a difference in your work?

If you joined pharmacy, you probably chose this profession because you enjoy helping others. Unfortunately, I'll bet you feel like you don't get to help others enough. If you answered yes to this question, then it's time for you to make new decisions about how you can make an impact.

Do you agree that what you've done in the past will not get you to where you want to be?

If you want to change your current situation, then you need to make new and different choices to move in a new direction.

Are you willing to challenge the negative beliefs that keep you where you are?

Do you accept that your current mindset needs to change?

Your thoughts are the genesis of every action. You wouldn't be where you are today if you didn't think it first. However, if you feel unfulfilled in your work, that's a result of your thinking, too. To change your situation, you need to have a new way of thinking to tackle new problems. Start by recognizing how much is possible for you.

Your potential could influence thousands of lives. If you aren't operating to your fullest, it means you are doing the world a disservice. Your audience is waiting for you to serve them with your passion, love, and happiness. The question is: **what's stopping you?** It's time to look directly into the fear, discomfort, resistance, and anything else that holds you back.

Your career end goal should be clearer by now. You know the destination... or at least you have an idea of what kind of work you wish to be doing. So how can you get to the other side? The gap between where you are now and where you want to be may seem impossible to bridge, or it may give you a ton of anxiety, but trust me, we will get you there. Section three will share strategies to rid yourself of these limiting beliefs and the other obstacles impeding you from where you want to go.

PART THREE

CLEAR YOUR WAY

"Just change course," you might think with an eye roll, "yeah, okay, Alex. No problem." I get it. I probably said the same thing a hundred times before I finally made the leap. That's because of that little voice, ego, peppering my thinking with words of resistance and caution. *Stay away from the things that seem hard or heart-stoppingly terrifying. Stick where you're comfortable, where things are easy.* I listened to my ego for years.

I chose pharmacy because it was the most accessible path out there. I wanted someone else to decide for me what career path would be the easiest and then I wanted to stay put. When I was in pre-pharmacy school, I remember telling myself: "You've tried to switch majors so many times, but for one reason or another, you remain in pre-pharmacy. This program may be difficult, but you seem to maintain good grades. Keep trying."

I continued to believe this lie because I was also unsuccessful at changing careers within pharmacy. The difficulties of switching were too much to handle. I wanted to avoid the conflict of handling career counselors, discussions with my mom, and changing classes at my college. I admit that my pride also made me stick with it. My ego did other things to keep me where I was, too, like making me feel good about myself at the expense of others.

One particularly awful conversation still stands out in my memory. I had a friend in pre-pharmacy who didn't make the cut for our pharmacy school's program. She re-applied the following year, the same year I applied. After I found out we both had been accepted into the program, we were chatting about the coming challenge and, for some idiotic reason, I asked, "So will you sit with the other failure students who didn't make it in last year's cut?"

CRINGE MOMENT.

This is the stuff I wake up to think about at two a.m.

Luckily, I realized my total blunder and apologized for my arrogance to my fellow Ferris bulldog. Then I took a good hard look at my ego.

My ego made me feel elevated. Every time a fellow pre-pharmacy student dropped out, I felt temporarily sorry for them, but later would boost myself and say things like, "Look at you, Alex, you've outlasted the failures." With each accomplishment or snippet of recognition I received, the higher I felt... and the more fragile my ego became. I couldn't risk failure or admit that I made a mistake—my ego couldn't handle that! So I kept my head down and stayed busy. My actions had brought me to where I was, and my ego worked hard to ensure I stayed put.

This is how we live day to day. We busy ourselves with a dead-end job, Netflix series, hobbies, and rarely look up to see the direction we go. We live with regrets. We don't do the things we desperately want to do. We live vicariously through others who achieve the things we wish we could. And we ignore our agency, our power to make our own choices and see them through.

This is your warning call to look up. What obstacles—internal or external—are impeding your path, and **are you ready to move them out of your way**?

WHAT ARE YOU AFRAID OF?

Erika was a client who hired me to help her get out of a hospital job. We got off to a great start, but about two to three weeks into our coaching sessions, I noticed she wasn't following up on her action steps. I confronted her with a compelling (but uncommonly asked) question: "What's stopping you from taking action?"

Erika's response didn't shock me. She began with a story about how she should be happy and how she felt guilty about her discontent. She thought she should be satisfied with her life even though she desperately wanted out of her job. I pressed her with a few more questions, and Erika revealed an underlying fear: once she finished her assigned action steps, people would notice that she was making a change in her life. She didn't want their unnecessary attention.

"Look," I told her, "if you're trying to find a new job, you better hope someone notices. If no one notices, then you'll never get a referred to a new position!"

Our call continued but, as we neared the end of our session, something was still bugging me. We had spoken for over an hour, but I felt as though we hadn't unearthed the real reason Erika was holding herself back. I pried more into her desire to avoid attention, and that's when she told her truth. She was afraid her father would find out that she was looking for a new job. "Why don't you want that?" I asked.

Erika poured out her fears in response to my question. She would probably have to move away from her current area and that would mean she wouldn't see her dad as often. Her father loved her but didn't have a good way to communicate his feelings, so he would berate Erika if she brought up how much she hated her position. Her father didn't want her to be unhappy, but for him, being unhappy in a career was a regular part of everyday life. Erika didn't want to accept that, but she still needed to communicate to her dad that she loved him and wanted his approval to seek a new position.

It's anyone's guess what's stopping you from living the life you've always wanted.

Maybe you think your spouse will judge you.

Maybe you believe no one will support you.

Maybe you don't believe you deserve to have what you want.

Maybe you'll fail.

Whatever fear you have about your goals, it will do its best to keep you stuck.

Fear is a natural and healthy thing to have; in fact, it's integral to human survival. Fear drove us to fight or flight when faced with a deadly situation. There was a third response, too: freeze. You're unlikely to encounter a mountain lion, but you still have the same fear responses hardwired into your brain as your cavemen ancestors.

Fear keeps you safe. Unfortunately, fear also holds you back in your comfort zone. Fear protects you from failure, public speaking, looking stupid, rejection, constructive feedback, and many situations that could benefit you. I help people overcome fear. Anyone can overcome these things, but what determines your success is how willing you are to be uncomfortable. That's what Part Three is all about. Let's talk about what scares you.

Name Your Fears

"How long have you dealing with this?" I asked. "I've been beating myself up since I was a child," she answered. Elena and I were working together on helping her transition into medical affairs. In one session, as we discussed her action steps, she shared how she was distracted lately. I asked why and found out she was waking up in the middle of the night multiple times every night. She bluntly stated, "I ask myself questions like, 'Something is off, what did I do wrong?' or 'What could I have done differently?'"

These thoughts weren't just about her career transition, it was about everything: conversations at work and with her in-laws, and decisions with her family. She shared that her thoughts constantly plague her with what-if scenarios. "I've been doing this for decades," she said. Elena's voice sounded strained, like she was holding back tears.

I asked, "When did this all start?" "Since I was a child," she answered. During her childhood, she grew up in a traditional Indian home. She was the firstborn, and in her household, this was a bad thing. Her grandfather purported that the firstborn should have been a boy, and nothing good would come from her. She aimed to prove them all wrong, by going to college, getting her PharmD degree, and having a successful career. Despite being quite accomplished, her never-ending self-doubt caused Elena stress and anxiety every day. "How have you tried to combat this mental habit?" I asked. She replied that she had not yet found a successful strategy.

Your fear holds you tightly in your comfort zone, far away from your zone of genius. Elena's negative thoughts kept her from taking action in her career. The first step to overcome fears is to acknowledge them. Fear likes to be amorphous. One minute, your fear will tell you that you'll never succeed; the next minute it says you'll fail once you achieve a small amount of success. A classic example I see is my clients receiving a job offer (the very thing they've worked so hard to achieve) only to fear they will fail at the job once they start. They're always surprised to learn that plenty of others grapple with the same anxiety. You, too, maybe be surprised by how much your fear diminishes once you pull it out of your head.

So name your fear. Write it down. What's the fear saying? You fear may sound like

- No one will give me a chance

- There's no way I can find a job in your town

- What if people think I'm stupid for saying this?

You take away fear's power by putting it down on the page. It's like you strike a nail through fear's amorphous body, stopping it from changing into another fear. I like to ask next: **"What's the worst possible thing that could happen if the fear comes true?"** Often the answer is, "Nothing consequential. I could bounce back from this failure."

Stepping into an indispensable career means taking risks, looking foolish, and facing fear and possibly rejection. Simply writing your fears down won't stop them from coming back. You need a strategy to overcome your worry when the fear pops up again.

Overcome Roadblocks

Fear will stop you at some point. Becoming indispensable means taking risks. You have to "put yourself out there" to get noticed by your next employer or customer. Being willing to become great at what you are means others will judge you. They'll see you differently. Unless you're ready for this change, it will slow you down. It's not a matter of *if* roadblocks happen, but *when*. You may not think it will, but it'll show up somehow. You'll distract yourself with entertainment or a new side project, or you'll redouble efforts at your job. Fear wants to keep you "safe." Let's go step by step what to do the next time fear stops you in your career strategy. Then we will walk through a real example of how I use the following five steps. I learned this approach from Gay Hendricks and have adapted the process here:

1. Identify the fear.

2. Turn your focus elsewhere.

3. Ask yourself, "What's the new positive thing coming into being?"

4. Focus on the new thing and all the emotions it causes.

5. Reflect later on the new thing and the cause of the worry.

Let's start at the beginning

Identify the Fear: An all-too-common fear most pharmacists have when transitioning is money. Money is often reported as the thing holding us back from all sorts of decisions, especially career transitions. I have the same fear. As I write this, I transitioned into my business full time. My business is now the sole income for my family. Because of this, I receive all sorts of fearful doubts about my inability to provide.

Around September 2017, my financial fears were getting so bad that I knew the reason why I stopped growing my business was because I was afraid of failure. I was afraid that if I made more money, I would get big-headed and think I could live off the business (counter-intuitive I know). I was afraid my ego would lead me to make a scary decision: quit my day job and live off my business. Rather than work at an easy job 8 to 5 and get a paycheck every two weeks, I would be solely responsible for my family's well-being—and that terrified me. One day, while at work, I remember feeling anxious about the decision to make my business full time (a feeling similar to what my clients feel when making a transition, potentially to something that may earn them less money). I acknowledged my fear and wrote it down in my daily planner: "I'm afraid I will fail my family, specifically our financial needs."

Writing down my fear helped keep me from the frantic thinking that leads to even more awful thoughts like, "You'll fail to grow your business. You'll have to go back to your old job. You'll hate the future you're creating. Everyone will know you're a hack and failure…" and so on. Fear loves to spiral your mind into something bigger like anxiety.

Immediately after writing down this fear, I turned my focus away from it.

Turn Your Focus Elsewhere: I put this worry into an imaginary ball and throw it away. Literally. Sounds weird, right? I found it weird at first, too, but it helps to shift my focus by doing something physical. Then I can reset my thinking to something more constructive. It's as if I'm telling my brain to move away from fear to hope. Simply telling myself, "Stop thinking these negative thoughts" works about as well as telling yourself to not think about a pink elephant. You're thinking about a pink elephant now, right? But shifting the mind away from fear to the new thing that's coming into being works like a charm. Move your body, do an exercise, or simply mentally throw it away if you can't physically shift your focus away.

Ask yourself, "What's the new positive thing coming into being?": I ask myself, "What's the new positive thing coming into being?" I verbalize the question and begin jotting down the different things I am excited about in my business. I write down:10,000 pharmacists become inspired to pursue a new and happy career path

- 100 new pharmacy tech companies are born and employing new pharmacists thanks to my mentoring efforts

- By 2019, the business funds two family adoptions ($50K total)

- My business makes more than enough and we live off 20% of the income, giving or investing 80% of the rest. Looking at that list makes me feel MUCH better.

If you write down or say things that are negative, then you haven't shifted your focus away from fear yet. This is a common occurrence because your brain developed its fear habit years ago. Your brain is fighting a new way of thinking by imagining fearful outcomes. Revisit step two. Shift your focus away and ask the question again.

Focus on the new thing and all the emotions it causes: As I wonder these things, I focus on where in my body I feel this excitement. I'm not a mushy-gooey touchy-feely kind of guy, which you've probably picked up by now. *Logan*, starring Hugh Jackman, was the last movie I cried at (at the end of course... no spoilers). Despite my ego and avoidance of pseudoscience, I've learned that our emotions influence every decision we make. You could argue that you make logical decisions, but economic, psychological, and health research offer strong evidence that we are emotional decision-makers. Just think about all the people who don't take their medications as prescribed. Logically, their health should be a top priority, but people don't reason logically. We skip exercise routines, avoid difficult conversations, hit the snooze button, binge on Netflix series, or go on buying sprees.

To solidify a move in a new direction, away from fear, I've found it helpful to focus emotionally on the new direction with my body. I feel a swelling in my chest when I get excited, so I'll focus on this feeling as long as I can. I don't think about anything else. I enjoy the moment, savoring every second of my excitement. Occasionally, I'll shed a tear because I get overly excited about what will happen.

Reflect after the exercise on the cause and new direction: Either the next day or later the same day I will reflect on this experience. If all went well, I won't relapse into fear.

My new direction will drive me forward, and I'll be focused on my task at hand. But occasionally I'll slip back into fear and be driven to inaction. In these cases, I've found it's because I skipped a step or didn't fully address the worry. When I skip, it's usually because I tell myself something like, "Okay, you've moved past this fear, time to focus on the next thing." I don't enjoy the positive feeling as long as I can. I rush the process, and eventually my emotions will turn back to my fear and I'll have to repeat the five steps all over again. In my example, I later reflected on the cause of my fear. I noted that what kickstarted my financial anxiety was reviewing my credit card payment. My wife typically handles the payments, but I was reviewing finances of the business and noticed a larger than normal credit card bill past its payment due date. My wife and I reviewed all our major purchases before buying, so none of the purchases were a surprise to me, but the total amount was a jaw-dropper. It stirred up an emotional, fearful question, "Can you really do entrepreneurship if you're messing up *now*, even when you have two sources of income?"

I realized that the fear was only caused by the amount of the credit card payment and resolved myself to be adamant about paying credit cards on time, as to avoid late fees and large sums from accruing. Megan agreed and vowed to support paying off the credit cards monthly. What about your fears? It isn't a matter of *if*, but *when*. A roadblock will appear to stop you from progress. A distraction will pop up to halt you from emailing a manager. An interruption, disguised as an opportunity, will appear. Your brain will do just about anything to create an escape from addressing your fears— even convince you that your fears are entirely rational. Can you commit to overcoming those "practical" fears?

FINANCES AND FAILURE: TACKLING YOUR PRACTICAL FEARS

Fear likes to change its shape. One minute we're worried about hating our jobs, the next we stress about the price of gas and war with North Korea. Those fears are pretty easy to see. But what about the ones we don't recognize as fear? What do we do when fear masquerades as common sense?

Let's take a look at the two "practical" fears I see most often when helping my clients move into more fulfilling work: finances and failure.

Finances

Reed was a pharmacist who faced an unfortunate turn of career events. After multiple job transitions, his latest job created so much stress that it had made him anxious and depressed. Reed was at his wit's end, which is how he ended up on the phone with me. After speaking for over two hours, Reed came face to face with a painful truth: He was stuck in his job because of his lifestyle. He had a huge mortgage, college loans ($150,000, if memory serves me), a car payment, a boat payment, extravagant vacations to the world's most exotic locations, and credit card balances that would make anyone cringe. He couldn't transition into a new job because almost all of the open positions paid less than his current one. In order to change his career around, he would have to make sacrifices he wasn't willing to make.

Reed isn't alone. Thousands of pharmacists (and other high-income earners) get trapped in their jobs by their financial choices—many of them made unintentionally. It's common practice to "buy what you can afford," and so pharmacists live up to their spending limit and beyond. We create golden handcuffs to jobs that make us miserable.

Are your finances keeping you trapped? Given what I've seen in my work with my clients, money is the main reason most pharmacists stay in jobs they hate. Living freely means you can do the things you love without the burden of money needs—but first, you need to figure out what stands in your way.

> Is your debt manageable on a lower income? What is holding you back from being free financially?
>
> If you could get rid of a monthly payment, could you step into a new career that paid less? How could you eliminate expenses to do work you would enjoy more?

Look for opportunity. Where can you make a change? Once you've identified your financial barriers, it's time to figure out what you can do about them. What can you change, reduce, or give up entirely? While it may seem like getting rid of Netflix won't make much of difference, small changes like this can add up. A friend and fellow pharmacist, Phillip, shared how he transitioned from living paycheck to paycheck to eliminating expenses and investing the difference. He and his wife used all their income once they started working, until, after about two years of this lifestyle, they had a "come-to-Jesus moment" with their budget. They were dinged twice on a late credit card payment, which was a pattern, and it stopped them from getting a loan on a house they wanted. Phillip and his wife eliminated most of their subscription services, like Netflix, Blue Apron, and a few clothing subscriptions. They found cheaper ways to buy food, and did all the typical recommendations from frugal money blogs. (I recommend the *YourFinancialPharmacist.com* blog for strategies if you need them.) They shaped up and addressed their poor spending habits, eliminated a lot of their frivolous spending, and limited their budgets to allow for the things they wanted. After buckling down, they created over $2,000 monthly to invest into the stock market. Investing now is smart and practical, but it assumes that you will be working a job you love the entirety of your career. I would never prescribe you invest your monies now if you hate (or even just "deal with") your work. Don't let your financial priorities stop you from pursuing excellence in your career. Not investing for six months may hurt your retirement nest egg or your kid's college fund, but to spend that money now on a career transition into something you're passionate about would never be something you'd regret. Or maybe you'd rather get rid of your loans ASAP like me. While I believe in the power of investing now and reaping later, my wife and I prioritized freedom over investing. If we chose to immediately invest more versus paying off debt, I wouldn't have been able to become debt free and leave my job as soon as we planned. Yes, we're losing out on reaping a larger benefit later in life, but we don't plan on retiring. I'd rather create a life I love now than work a job I slog through until I'm 70.

The financial decision is yours and it should be based on your priorities, not on FOMO (fear of missing out). Don't let the fear of missing out on creature comforts or investing now stop you from enjoying a new job. There's no sense in becoming a prisoner to your plan for financial freedom

Failure: The Practical Excuse for Not Trying

"Why aren't you selling your product?" I texted Gene, a pharmacist and budding tech entrepreneur. He had an informatics residency and developed software for the hospital. The hospital wanted rights to the software and bought it for a low-end five-figure deal. He wanted my help to grow his business so he could sell his software to more hospitals and eventually make his software company his main gig. Gene avoided selling conversations with prospects, and he knew it. He shared that he wasn't confident in his product and felt like it needed more development: a perfectionist's excuse for avoiding failure. He replied to my question with, "I would sell it happily… But I think it's a confidence issue on my part. Even though I have no reason not to be." He isn't alone. Everyone is scared of failure or rejection. The best way to overcome this barrier is to expect failure and practice your response to it.

Expect Failure. Your path to success will be marked with failures and you should seek them often. I should clarify, I don't mean to try to fail, but rather *expect* failure. Growing your pharmacy career isn't the same as patient care. A life doesn't hang in the balance. You can afford failure. Don't have high hopes that everything will work out in your journey. It almost never does. I can't tell you how many times I've disappointed clients, customers and others. I can't tell you how many times I've invested in other people and they eventually disappoint me. I've learned that failure will happen along my path. It's about what you do after you fail that determines your trajectory. Your reaction to that failure is what will determine your success. You likely will fail, but it's taking what you learned from your experiment and moving forward. If you need a little inspiration, I suggest you consider learning from an infant.

A parent's proudest moments are when their kids overcome a major obstacle or accomplish a feat, and one of the first is the ability to walk. My oldest daughter Izzie took her time reaching this milestone. I remember secretly condemning my "poor" parenting skills as I compared her progress to other children, worried that I was doing something wrong. I looked to blame my wife for the problem, too—probably out of a selfish desire to share the weight of this "failure." One day, during my residency rotations, I got the call. "She's walking! And it's beautiful." That night I traveled home to watch my little girl take wobbly steps across the living room. Pride swelled in me.

Walking is a big leap forward for a baby. It's her first taste of freedom and agency. She can move almost anywhere whenever she wants. No limitations, other than barriers taller than herself. Izzie's world just got a lot bigger. I know you can't recall the details of when you learned to walk, but let's do a thought experiment. Go back to when your mom or dad helped you take your first steps. What might they have said to you? What tone did they use? Did you feel safe? Supported? Encouraged?

Did you doubt yourself? Were you questioning your every move? Did you try to convince yourself that the ground was a much safer place to stay than upright on your wobbly legs? (It is.) Did you justify your decision not to learn to walk because walking could lead to horrible accidents or awkward situations? Did you argue with yourself that until your movement is perfect, that's when you'll start walking?

Of course not.

Children don't doubt their ability. They pursue their goals with a hilarious amount of gusto. My youngest daughter Addie doesn't know the meaning of "no." Despite how many times I tell her, "No cookies," she comes up with reasons why she should have a treat, like, "I'm good girl today, so I need to have cookie now." Why can't we do that as adults? What happened? We were born fearless, and "reality" hit us in the face during childhood. We became these coward creatures who are so fearful of what could happen that we never act.

A friend of mine kept himself away from the dating scene because he feared getting hurt again. I sympathize with him; I'm no stranger to heartbreak. But pain comes with the territory. Passion derives from a Greek word, *pathéma*, which means to suffer. I'm passionate about my wife, but our marriage has been full of struggles, sadness, and suffering. We've fought plenty. I've sacrificed some of my desires to be with the woman of my dreams. My friend will never find a spouse with a fear-based mentality.

Isn't it funny how we reason with our fear? We give ourselves plenty of logical reasons not to pursue what we want:

> Others will think I'm weird or out of line.

> What if nobody likes what I create?

> I'll fail, so why even try?

I need to keep my pharmacy job. I'll disappoint everyone if I quit.

I can't leave this job. I'll lose everything.

You didn't worry like that when learning how to walk. You never considered the fall. Your natural reaction was to get up and try again. Can you tap back into that mindset? Can you set your fears to the side and step forward? Can you get back up after a fall? Overcoming this "practical" fear requires a bit of grit.

Build your resilience: A hundred and fifty years ago, experts thought women would die if they were on a train that went faster than 50 mph. A cultural anthropologist named Genevieve Bell told the *Wall Street Journal* that critics of train innovation thought "women's bodies were not designed to go at 50 miles an hour," and worried that "[female passengers'] uteruses would fly out of [their] bodies as they were accelerated to that speed." I'm happy that one woman, decades ago, was brave enough to go against "experts" and prove them wrong.

Limitations on the human condition are constantly being broken. The six-minute mile was thought to be impossible to breark. Traveling to the moon was thought impossible for millennia. Those who break past those limitations share one thing: grit. *Grit*, defined by leading research expert Angela Duckworth, is a perseverance and passion for long-term goals. Grit means following through on what you say you'll do. Grit is having the courage to ask despite what others say or think. Grit is having optimism in the face of adversity and chasing excellence over perfection.

The good news is that you can improve your grit to become more resilient in the face of failure. Research performed by

Angela Duckworth, available in her book, *Grit: The Power of Passion and Perseverance*, found that grit was a character quality that could improve. And she found an exercise to help students improve their ability to achieve long-term goals.

The exercise is called the If-Then Plan, and it's so simple I can run through it with my young daughters:

> IF I run into X problem,
>
> THEN I will do Y

This plan helps you identify and overcome likely roadblocks on your path to success. Here are some example If-Then plans:

> IF I struggle with sleeping in (instead of working on my career action steps),
>
> THEN I will place my alarm 15 feet from my bed so I must get up.
>
> IF I become distracted on Facebook
>
> THEN I will use the Facebook newsfeed eradicator on Google Chrome.

Angela Duckworth found that those who plan around their potential problems were more like to accomplish their goals. By implementing this plan, you will become grittier. In other words, you're more likely to overcome your practical fears and succeed.

OVERCOME WEAKNESSES, FAILURES, AND REJECTIONS

As we've established, I am not mechanically inclined. After coming home from our honeymoon, my wife and I spent hours putting together our new apartment. I spent 30 minutes trying to build our vacuum. The blasted thing pitted its will against mine—and it would not come together no matter what I tried. I nearly threw the contraption out the window. Shortly after my frustrated fit, my wife had it running within a minute.

No matter what I do, I cannot figure things out with my hands. I cannot solve simple mechanical problems. I lose at Jenga™ nine times out of ten. A mechanical pencil is my worst nightmare. I've learned to accept it and focus my efforts where I can excel.

Working on every one of your weaknesses will not improve your career or create more fulfillment. Frankly, it would waste a lot of your time. Sometimes the best thing you can do is accept the things you cannot change and put your energy elsewhere. I'm honestly happy that I don't have to count pills because I would mess up my count. I had to double-count my pills all the time during my community pharmacy internship, so much so that I was often booted from the line and placed on customer duty or restocking the shelves. It doesn't help that I'm slightly dyslexic with numbers. Whenever a customer or RN would call in the pharmacy and report a number, I had to ask them four times to repeat it because I can't write numbers down quickly. They get jumbled up in my mind.

That said, what I want to share with you is how to overcome any failure, rejection, or new weakness found. I learned this technique through parenting.

My eldest daughter is a wonderful, beautiful, and caring girl. She's also prone to outbursts of tremendous terror screams when she doesn't get her way. One morning, in particular, exemplifies this behavior.

My youngest daughter, Addie, wanted to watch herself singing in the Christmas program, so I gave her my phone and let her watch while eating breakfast. While I was changing my clothes, my oldest daughter, Izzie, came to the table and also wanted to see the video. Because every human is born selfish, Addie didn't want Izzie to see the video and didn't share the phone. Suddenly, of course, I hear cries of despair from Izzie. I walk into the room and immediately went into dad-mode to do some damage control.

I realized that this was a great teaching moment for my daughter. I began to ask her some questions:

What happened at the table? Izzie told me everything that Addie did to ruin her day. In Izzie's mind, Addie made it the worst day ever.

Without judging her, I accepted those "facts." *Okay, how did you feel when that happened?* My goal was to get her talking without questioning whether she was "right" to feel the way she did. When we don't express what our feelings are, we can't accept the situation for what it is and get on with how to solve the situation. If I were to rush to my next question without addressing her emotions, Izzie wouldn't be able to handle moving on with the situation because she feels hurt. This powerful approach is one I learned from *Seven Habits of Highly Effective People* by Stephen Covey: first understand, and then be understood. We have to seek to understand someone before having them trying to understand us. We naturally want to be understood first because we are human beings. My daughter shared how frustrated she felt that Addie didn't share with her. It made her mad enough to say: "I wish she would go away." Again, I learned not to judge her and say things like, "You shouldn't wish that." or "Never say that again," as I had done in the past. Instead, I asked her a new question: *What would you do differently if Addie doesn't share with you again?*

This new question opened up my daughter's creativity. She began telling how she would try to get Addie to say "yes." She knows that I talk a lot about influence and motivation in our home. She's learned that if you know what motivates other people, that you can get them to help you do anything. Izzie shared her ideas with me:

> "I could give her a piece of my muffin to share with me." "Good idea, Izzie."

> "If she doesn't share again, then I can go to you and ask for help." "Excellent."

> "I could look at the video later when she isn't looking at it." "Wow, Izzie, you could do that."

> Then I help her bring it all together with an action plan. *What will you do next time?*

How many times have you advised a friend or family member, and you know it's the best advice out there. It's simple what to do in your mind. And yet, for whatever reason, this person doesn't follow your advice. How could they be so foolish? You know exactly what to do, but they don't seem to trust you.

Izzie created her action plan—and she felt more inclined to follow it because **the plan was hers**, not my plan.

Following your own plan is so much easier than following someone else's. This is the power of coaching. I don't tell anyone what to do. I may offer suggestions as to what their options are, but all my clients make decisions on their own, and I just hold them accountable to their choices, which in turn makes them more confident to explore their careers. The best way to foster confidence in the face of fear is to make your own decision, rather than following what you're told what to do. You don't need more information to make a decision. As Derek Sivers, founder of CD Baby, once said,

"If [more] information was the answer, then we'd all be billionaires with perfect abs."

You don't need more information right now. You need to make a decision.

This four-step line of questioning allows you to evaluate your failures and create a new action plan to avoid failure.

What happened?

What did that make you feel?

What would you have done differently?

What will you do next time?

Doing this process will make you "failure-proof"—not in the sense that you'll never experience failure (it's impossible to be human and not fail), but you'll be immune to what failure can do to people: keep them trapped in their comfort zone. Your comfort zone is where careers die. Once people fail, they want to stay where failure isn't possible. It creates a safe space where you don't want to try harder to escape the rat race.

Are You Trapped in Your Safe Space?

For the longest time, I thought I was ugly. I had acne in high school—not the severe form that you'd see in acne product commercials, but bad enough to affect my self-image. I remember waking up every day looking at myself in the mirror and think, "You are not easy to look at. Who's gonna think you're attractive?" I lacked confidence in my appearance, so I relied on my humor to charm my way to the top. For a long time, I thought dating wasn't achievable. "No one will date you" I thought, and so I didn't date until my senior year of high school.

I created a self-fulfilling prophecy. I believed no one would date me, so I never pursued a girlfriend. And because I didn't have a girlfriend, I thought no one would date me.

I hear similar beliefs from pharmacists every week:

> *"I can't leave my job."*

> *"There are no jobs available."*

> *"We can't move to find a new job."*

> *"My boss wouldn't allow me to do that."*

147

These statements have one thing in common: they originate from the mind.

Let's dissect that first thought, "I can't leave my job." Why can't you leave your job? Are you bound by a land-contract that says you will lose your firstborn son if you negate the deal? Did you agree to any Faustian bargains? No? Okay then. What is the worst possible outcome if you left your job?

Well, I'd have to find another one.

Okay. What's wrong with that?

It's impossible! There are no jobs out there. And the ones that are available are garbage.

If there are no jobs out there, then why don't we have more unemployed pharmacists? Why aren't more pharmacy schools shutting down? Why don't we hear about more pharmacists joining different professions? Why do you have a job if there are no jobs available? *Well, it is possible. But it's tough.*

Whatever level of difficulty you have in your mind must mean that you are afraid of failure or rejection. We place ourselves in our own mind prisons. Whatever beliefs we have about our situation are fulfilled by our actions.

You can change jobs. You could do whatever you try. You may not make it, but if you give it your best effort, then you can know that even if you fail, you have the satisfaction of trying. And then you can try something else.

Real failure is giving up. Failure is the pharmacist who hates his life, hates his job, lets everyone else know about his frustration, and does nothing to change his situation. A failed career is one with no joy, love, or satisfaction. The first step to break free from it is to identify what scares you most. The second step is to practice doing that thing.

"Can I Borrow Your Dog?"

"Can I borrow your dog?" It's not a question I (or anyone else) ask every day. But there I was on a porch in my hometown, asking a stranger if I could borrow his best (furry) friend.

You see, as much as I like to give off a confident self-image, I have as much doubt and fear as the next guy. As a struggling business coach in 2014, I knew that my lack of confidence in my ability to sell was resulting in losing contracts. I listened to a TED talk from a guy named Jia Jiang, who did a 100-day rejection challenge. The challenge made him internet famous, and he eventually wrote a book called *Rejection Proof.* Inspired by his story and wanting to overcome my lack of confidence, I decided to do the same thing, and turned the idea into a podcast.

I called my podcast "The 66-Day Experiment." The idea was based on a study done by the University College of London that demonstrated that it takes 66 days to form a habit. I had multiple habits I wanted to do, like read and exercise more. The first season was all about reading one book every day. Yes, I speed-read one book every day for 66 days, plus or minus a few days. I believe I read about 56 books over the span of 66 days. Season Two's challenge was grappling with rejection.

And that's how I found myself standing at the door of a complete stranger, asking him if my family and I could walk his dog.

"What?" he asked.

So I unconfidently asked again. "Would you mind if we borrowed your dog for a walk?" The man was right to be puzzled by such an odd request. I stood on his front porch, with my wife and kids behind me—and I believe it was their smiling faces that kept him from shutting the door in my face. "Well, what will you do with her?" he asked.

I bluntly replied, "My wife really wants a dog, and so do my kiddos. So I thought it would be interesting to 'try out' a dog. We will walk around the block for a few minutes, but I promise we won't be gone longer for fifteen."

"Um, okay then. Yeah. Sure." He grabbed the dog's leash, told us her name and a few pointers on walking her properly. A minute later, we were walking a dog and laughing our heads off. Fear stops you from stepping outside your comfort zone. The pain of doing something different is overwhelming at times, enough to trap you where you are. But it's the relief (and sometimes the laughter) on the other side of the pain where freedom exists. Escaping your comfort zone will set you free to try new things, explore your zone of genius, and make new connections. In the next part, I will introduce strategies that require bravery from you. The strategies work. But you must be willing to step outside your comfort zone. I learned from this experiment that rejection is not as painful as it seems. By turning my fear into something I practiced doing, I removed its hold over me.

Knock Out Your Obstacles

You more than likely are shaking your head, thinking, "It's not the same. Borrowing a dog is one thing, Alex. But you don't know my boss..." You're right. There isn't much that

I can say to change your negative thoughts. Could I ask you a question?

What if you didn't believe those excuses? What if you refused to believe that your boss was against you? What if you changed the way you thought about your current job? Could you accept the fact that your current job is a stepping stone to your next one? Could you reject the idea that you're too old, or too young, or you lack experience, or the job market is too saturated?

How can you meet the needs of your current company? What do your company emails focus on? What's important to them? You more than likely have ignored these messages because they repeat themselves or you thought they contained little useful information—until now.

What are others refusing to do? How could you volunteer your unique ability to improve the situation?**What if you refused to believe that you'd fail if you tried?** What kind of person could you become?

What are you avoiding or ignoring? Tim Ferriss asks a brilliant question in his book *The Four-Hour Work Week*: Are you inventing actions to avoid what is important? The brilliance of this question pinpoints how you could be avoiding doing something outside your comfort zone.

It's normal to avoid taking action on things that scare us. I love this question so much that I set it as an iPhone reminder twice a day. I ignore it occasionally, but when I do see it, I ask myself, "Am I really working on the thing I should be working on?" I don't have to ask the question if I'm on YouTube or Facebook. I know what I'm doing wrong, and I quickly jump back into the important task.

Your Negative Feedback May Hold the Answer

My fourth year of pharmacy school was more difficult than I anticipated. Not because I couldn't clinically perform, but because of personal interactions. Nearly every rotation I had, I received the same slice of feedback: you are arrogant.

Those words landed like a haymaker, but there was truth in their feedback. I needed to hear it because, at the time, I treated people like a means to my ends. But tucked away in that feedback was an important quality about myself that I was being told to hide: confidence. I realized one day, after listening to a podcast about self-improvement, that my negative feedback highlighted a strength of mine. Now, I use my confidence to do "crazy" things. I record myself regularly on my phone, my video camera, and send people videos of myself talking to them. It was weird at first, but now I'm a natural. And my clients love it! I regularly get messages that say: "First time ever receiving a video thank you message. Pretty awesome! Thank you!!!"

What negative feedback have you received? I'll bet you didn't see it as something that could transform into a strength. Maybe it's time to switch your perspective. Have you asked yourself before: What does this "weakness" reveal about your character? How could you turn this weakness into your strength?

DEVELOP "NEW" STRENGTHS

Jacqy, a clinical pharmacist in Colorado, shared with me a story I've heard hundreds of times in different ways. It went something like this:

> I have multiple letters after my name. But these certifications mean nothing to me. I feel like I'm in an endless maze. I can't go up in the company; there's no room for improvement. I've been doing the same job for ten years and every day feels like Groundhog Day—except this isn't a movie. It's is my real life. There is no escape, no happy ending. I'm terrified that I'll get stuck here for another 20 to 30 years.

The frustration in her voice was impossible to miss. It was clear she felt like she was on a treadmill and looking for ways off the spinning belt. She continued:

> There are hundreds of job options out there—but I don't know if pharmacy is even right for me. I feel like I should leave pharmacy altogether, but if I do, that means I've given up on my HUGE investment into my career. Wouldn't that make me a failure? What should my next step be? I worry that whatever action I take will be the wrong one. Or I'll choose a

business pursuit that'll tank after a few years. I feel like there is no right step forward.

Then came the question: *What do I do?* It's so tricky to declutter your mind and even more difficult to determine which path, among thousands, is best for you. That's when people get on the phone with me.

You Need Help

In Dr. Henry Cloud's excellent book, *The Power of the Other*, he describes what every person, but especially high-performing individuals need: **powerful positive relationships ("the other") that allow vulnerability**. Dr. Cloud shares the science and multiple stories of high-performing CEOs, superstars and athletes who grow through the power of the other. Each person follows a story trend: the person runs into a problem, avoids addressing the problem, attempts a solution which usually is temporary, then approaches Dr. Cloud to address the real problem, the power of the other. Dr. Cloud's premise is that something is required to experience a fulfilling life in general, not just in work. Vulnerable relationships with others are required to create the space to solve the real issues. A student in my Career Jumpstart class experienced this very problem. Sarah signed up for my class to learn more techniques on how to find a better pharmacy job. She didn't sign up for the coaching part of my program. I reach out to every new student and ask to chat with them to ensure their career search is going well. Sarah shared she had been looking for a job for a year and a half before she signed up. She outlined how she had applied to over four dozen jobs over the previous 18 months, had been volunteering for projects to grow her career experience, and had began to meet with people to grow her network opportunities. All great action steps, I concluded. After listening to a few modules of the Career Jumpstart course, she added more action steps to take. She thought those would help her move to the next step of her career. She then asked my opinion of her plan. "I like all of the steps you're taking," I told her. "They will definitely move you out of your comfort zone. However, there's a vital piece that's missing which likely will sabotage your plan." "What's missing?" she asked. "Well, over the last eighteen months you had searched diligently for a job, albeit not consistently." Sarah had previously told me how she went through phases of frantically applying to jobs only to give up for a time. Her job application phases, she admitted, were often based on negative emotions created from her day job. I explained, "Your efforts to find a new job are based on your personal energy. Whether you feel like working on your career or not determines the energy you put into it. And lately you admitted to not hustling the way you'd like to on your career, which is because of your current job. Your energy to put into this career transition is solely based on your performance, which has proven to fail you. What's missing is that you not relying on others to help you. "Sarah fell silent. She eventually started, "But I don't have friends that I can share this with. If I do talk about my struggles, I either get, 'It's okay, you'll eventually find something,' or 'I'm in the same boat as you.' Half of my friends hate their jobs just as much as I do. Whenever we meet, our conversations are about how much we hate our jobs. How can I find people who are willing to help me?"

I replied, "Well, you can start with me. A reason why I have a coach is because I need people to hold me accountable to my goals. I need people in my life who don't listen to my inner fear." I explained how I slowly removed people from my life who didn't create a positive energy toward the things I wanted. If a friend made fun of my entrepreneurial pursuits, I laughed it off, but grew slowly apart from them. I added people into my life who were like-minded, who want similar things, who wouldn't discourage me from pursuing abundance, and who needed the same encouragement I desperately need.

Mindset and action won't solve everything. You need other people to help you. Whether you want to admit it or not, you haven't made it this far without others.

It was easy for you to be vulnerable in pharmacy school. You weren't the expert. No one expected you to know the basics of being a pharmacist. Along the way, professors and pharmacists gave back to you. In your state of vulnerability, you learned from others how to be a pharmacist. Once graduated, you likely lost a mentor, or maybe you never had one. You no longer can be vulnerable because no one else acts this way at work. An unfulfilling career is likely to accompany a life without a mentor or support group. When a pharmacist comes to me for coaching, I'll ask about their support group or mentor, and many reply that they have no support, other than maybe a spouse. You couldn't have become a pharmacist without the support of others. Now it's time for you to find that support again. Whether through a coach, a mastermind group, or a friend, you need to have others encourage you when you feel at your worst.

Who Will Help You?

Mentor, coach, recruiter, fellow pharmacist. You need help. We all do. The old adage is true that your network determines your net worth. In this age of high competition, most job applications end up in the trash. I regularly speak with managers and recruiters who confirm the overabundance of applications for one job opening. Those invited to an interview are those who convinced the job interviewer they were trustworthy enough. Trust. The quality you need the most in their job market. Someone who can support you in a vulnerable relationship can come in a few forms:

- A *mentor* is someone who can listen to your situation and provide guidance that is usually based on his or her own experience. They want you to make the best decisions according to their knowledge, not yours. They do not understand how to truly find what makes you tick and how to move you into the next career.

- A *recruiter* is someone who will hold their cards close. While they are fantastic to include in your network, they have a job to do: find the *best* candidate for a job. They don't work for you; a recruiter works for a company. You likely are not always the best candidate. A recruiter will put his job before your opportunity to make a career transition.

- A *mastermind group* is a group of like-minded individuals who support the betterment of each member. Individuals are held to a standard of holding each other accountable to what they say they will do. I have the privilege of leading multiple masterminds over the last five years, and the personal benefits have been surprising.

- A *coach* is someone who provides support and guidance based on your situation (not his or hers). A coach is someone who helps you grow past what stops you in unexpected ways that often stick with you beyond the coaching session.

Building a professional support system is one of the strongest choices you can make for yourself. Naturally, I recommend you start with a coach.

Find a Coach

I help pharmacists create happy careers. Through coaching exercises, regular meetings, and courses, I provide pharmacists an outlet to strategize their career development into the next stage. Our clients meet with me, or another Happy PharmD coach, and we create a career development plan to move them into their next step. I never guarantee my clients will achieve success within a limited timeframe. I can't guarantee you'll find a job by following all the action steps in this book. However, what I can guarantee is that if you consistently follow my coaching program or this book, you will be able to create a valuable career.

I talk with at least five pharmacists every week who share a story similar to Jacqy's. If the pharmacist sounds like someone I can help, I invite them to a complementary coaching session with me so they can decide if it's an investment they want to make. If you've never considered coaching, now might be a good time.

Deep Inner Work

Early in my coaching career, a client named Daniel, who grew his business from $5,000 profit per month to $20,000 per month, told me something interesting in his testimony about my service:

"You'd think the extra money would be the thing most people would be thrilled about, but I'm more excited about the positive mental changes. I faced my own negativity for years. I would tell myself things like, 'No one will buy from you,' or 'You don't have enough credibility.' With Alex's coaching, I found myself telling myself a different story. I'm hopeful for the first about my business!"

I realized something deep about coaching then. People work with me to achieve an important result they want, but what they actually get at the end of coaching is something **life-changing**. Somewhere in my childhood, I earned a chip on my shoulder. The cause was a mixture of my father leaving when I was two and being adopted by a new dad when I was five. I continuously sought the rebel path. If everyone had to be quiet during class, I was the goofball standing on a desk when the teacher's back turned. The chip on my shoulder served me well. I felt driven to prove myself. My chip pushed me to work multiple jobs at once, excel in school, and graduate pharmacy school. As I ventured into the next area my chip would serve me, business, I again found myself driven by a need to prove myself. The funny thing is you can never have enough of what you don't really need. I'd spend 25 seconds celebrating an accomplishment, like graduating from pharmacy school, and then think about the next big thing to work on—the next way to prove myself. This cycle continued until I hired my first coach.

My coach helped me identify this struggle of proving myself. It manifests in different ways: beating myself up about not meeting a deadline, avoiding important work because I doubt my ability to do it well, the desire to look like I have it all together. My coach help me change the way I think.

I'm a completely different person from who I was five years ago. I don't think the same way, and thus I don't act the way I used to. My coach has helped me become the person I wanted to be, when my fears and doubts had stopped me from being that person. This deep inner change has created countless opportunities and saved myself from poor decisions. That's the power of coaching. A coach empowers you to overcome your personal struggles. Coaching helps you determine what is most important to you, to live a life consistent with your values, and to eliminate the limiting beliefs that create barriers to your progress. It is more than just support and good advice; coaching is a source of motivation and new perspectives, a jumpstart to my creativity, and a driver of action. Don't even get me started on the accountability factor. Most of all, the coaching I've received has been hugely empowering. There's power in knowing someone else believes in you, someone who won't listen to your negative thoughts and pushes you toward a big hairy audacious goal.

Coaching may be a good idea for you if:

- You're committed to make a change, but can't seem to actually follow through on your commitment

- You've tried for months to find a new job, but haven't found any success

- The companies you've interviewed at aren't calling back

- You're ready to fully work in your unique ability, but know the cards are stacked against you

- You want to try something new but don't have the confidenceYou're not sure where to start

You might be wondering, *"Should I spend money on coaching right now? What will be my return on investment?"* I can't answer that question for you. But what I do is provide a complementary, no-commitment, coaching session. I've found that when you experience coaching, you have an idea of how far it can push you forward. An investment in coaching is an investment in yourself and your future. Warren Buffett, one of the wealthiest people in the world, said, "Ultimately, there's one investment that supersedes all others: Invest in yourself," in a recent interview with Forbes. "Nobody can take away what you've got in yourself, and everybody has potential they haven't used yet."

What are you willing to invest in your unused potential? One dollar? One million dollars? Only you can decide how much you're willing to commit, where you'll invest your money, energy, and time, and how you'll define the ROI. You could spend $120,000 on additional certifications, degrees, and education, but if you do nothing with them (or continue to be miserable), then it's a lost investment. Let me be clear, though, about coaching. You do not need coaching. No one needs a coach. Plenty of pharmacists have successful careers without the help of a coach. The better question to ask yourself is, "Do you want a coach to push you into your zone of genius and the life you really want?"

I do. That's why I happily pay a coach to help me. A coach helps me grow beyond what I think is possible. My future is worth the investment. I think yours is, too.

What more would you be willing to pay to move toward a job that fulfills you?

Where Can You Be Better?

I'm a judgmental person. I've always compared myself to others. When I was a kid, I was always complaining to my parents about how everyone else had a Super Nintendo. Sadly, I also compared myself to those less fortunate than I was, and it made me feel better about myself. This became a habit over time, one I still battle to this day. I must constantly fight my ego, otherwise I run the risk of being an egotistical jerk. It is my worst fear, and yet I am drawn to that feeling.

When I first started my business, I compared myself to others who were further along, who had built more success and gained more recognition (and could demand higher fees). And that process never ends. I always hear about the success of others and think to myself, "Why can't I have that? What's wrong with me? What am I doing wrong?"

But there is a much stronger choice you can make: compare yourself to the person you used to be. Measure yourself by what you have done.

> Are you accomplishing more toward your goal?
>
> Did you build your career today?
>
> Did you improve your customer service?
>
> Are your more grateful?

Then compare yourself to who you want to become: Where can you be better?

This question alone is possibly your best career tool.

UNCOVER YOUR BEST HABITS

"You're just like your father." Five words that make my blood boil.

If you're married, you likely have had your significant other tell you that you are like your mother or father. And if you're like me, you've likely experienced an immediate blood pressure spike. Megan, my wife, is always right, and I know it. So I push harder against it.

"I am NOT like my father!" And the argument ensues.

I always want to be right. My father had the same habit. Arguing with my dad whenever we didn't see eye to eye became a habit. And now I argue with my wife. I still have to be right. I've carried this habit out of childhood into adulthood, my marriage, and even parenthood. Our habits will stick around until we decide to replace them with something better and, if we're not careful, they'll outlive us in our kids and the legacy we leave behind.

Aristotle said it best: "We are what we repeatedly do." We are our habits, and our habits make us. If you make it a habit to argue with everyone, then you will be known as a combative person. If you habitually compliment everyone, you'll likely be known as a likable person. Your habits led you to where you are today. "Success is not an act," Aristotle continues, "but a habit." Using your habits to push you into your next career move creates forward momentum, rather than pushing against the tides of change. Identifying your best habits will help you solidify your *indispensable* career path.

- **So, what are your best habits?**

- **What are your worst?**

- **What three habits are holding you back from reaching success?**

- **What three habits will bring you closer to what you want?**

These habits won't change easily, which is a good thing. In Part Four, we're going to dig into the proactive things you can do to shape your future self, your future career, and your future *life*. It's time to make yourself indispensable.

PART FOUR

BECOME INDISPENSABLE

"Amazon is going to change everything." I hear some version of this lamentation any time pharmacists discuss the future of our profession. While we can only speculate what Amazon will do, one thing is certain: change is coming.

But here's what a fear prisoner thinks:

> *Amazon will make our profession worse.*
>
> *Amazon will ruin community pharmacies. Thousands of pharmacists will be out of jobs.*
>
> *Pharmacists will suffer at the hands of Amazon.*

The fear prisoner expects the worst. She thinks only from a glass-half-empty perspective. She is reactive toward change, ready for the worst possible outcome.

Here's what the freed thinker expects:

> *What if I could work at Amazon as a pharmacist?*
>
> *What would I need to do to be considered at Amazon?*
>
> *How could I capitalize on Amazon's transition?*
>
> *Who will benefit from Amazon's move into pharmacy? How can I help those people?*
>
> *Who do I need to talk to about getting in on Amazon's game?*

The freed thinker continually innovates. She moves day to day with the comfort that all is right with the world, and when it isn't right, she creates a plan to make it so. When the freed thinker comes into a problem, she innovates her way out of the situation. She asks herself powerful questions to be creative. She develops a reputation as one who solves problems rather than one who complains about her issues.

If you believe you're a hardworking employee, then you'll behave like one. If you believe you hate your job and can't wait until closing time, then you'll behave like a person who hates his job. Your behavior reinforces your beliefs (whether positive or negative), and your thinking influences your actions. Your actions determine your path. The path to become an indispensable pharmacist is a proactive one.

So... who are you? Are you an unhappy pharmacist who wants a new job, or are you a proactive, indispensable pharmacist ready to take control?

The Proactive, Indispensable Pharmacist

The proactive pharmacist is one who follows her curiosity. She invests time during work and her evenings to expand her knowledge of a certain subject. She meets people who are doing new and exciting things in her space. She has a voice and knows no one can copy her. She wants to express her own opinion and does so by seeking opportunities to be heard, like conferences, online publications, colleges of pharmacy, and blogs. **The proactive pharmacist in engaged.**

The proactive pharmacist spends his morning commute listening to podcasts, audiobooks, and interviews about the latest and greatest perspectives on his interests. He expands his knowledge beyond his field. He knows he will create a new idea that will catch on, but until then, he'll keep on iterating. He suggests new ideas at work, knowing that others can contribute to his idea to make it even better. **The proactive pharmacist always seeks to be better.**

The proactive pharmacist doesn't allow herself to vegetate. She has a mind that doesn't shut off. She wakes up early Monday through Friday to build her idea. She goes out of her way to meet people who can help her, knowing they have abilities and knowledge she lacks and can propel her further down her path. Each idea she receives is rocket fuel to drive her. **The proactive pharmacist is excited, driven, and passionate.**

The proactive pharmacist knows where he is going with his career. He has a destination in mind and, though he doesn't know how he'll get there yet, he believes people will come along and help him reach his destination. **The proactive pharmacist sees a path.**

The proactive pharmacist has a big dream, and she knows it will take daily hustle to reach it. She puts in the time to build her dream. She accepts that she doesn't know what she's doing and is okay with looking a bit foolish. She knows taking one step at a time will get her closer every day. **The proactive pharmacist works for her future.**

The proactive pharmacist identifies where he wants his life to go. He doesn't let others make him do things he doesn't want to do. And if that happens, he creates a plan to escape. This pharmacist doesn't let life happen to him. **The proactive pharmacist makes himself indispensable.**

What Does It Mean to be Indispensable?

An indispensable career means your career holds value. Value is a skill, accomplishment, or zone of genius which a company is willing to pay you for—it's who you can help and how. It also speaks to how much it will cost to replace you. If you can be replaced by another pharmacist with a few months of training, then, by comparison, you do not hold much value. You are not indispensable. At least, not yet. Practically speaking, mostly any pharmacist can be replaced. However, the more unique your skills, abilities, and zone of genius, the less likely it is that companies will want to let you go and the more you'll be given opportunities to further display your greatness. The goal isn't to create an airtight career. The goal is to grow a career into one that inspires you. You'll never have 100% job security. The market could crash tomorrow. A nuclear holocaust can happen as I write these words... Perfect, I'm still here. The point is to build a career that makes it easy for you to find work that makes you happy. Work that challenges you and creates a sense of accomplishment. To become indispensable means being so valued by a company as to never lose employment. To become indispensable means your business idea is so valuable that people will throw money at it because it solves a problem.

Indispensable means you receive job offers from others, even when you aren't looking.

Indispensable means your reputation as a problem solver spreads.

Indispensable means opportunities are seen everywhere and your problem becomes selecting which problem to focus on.

Indispensable means your network is growing every week. Your relationships are meaningful, deeper than a LinkedIn connection.

At this point, you have an understanding of the job market, the problems of our pharmacy world, and what's holding you back from success. Let's focus on finding you opportunities to create an indispensable career.

Break It Down

There are two things you can focus on to create an indispensable career:

- Create relationships

- Create value

- All action steps forward will be aimed at these two goals.

Each of the following strategies and tips revolves around either relationships or value. Both are equally important and practically inseparable. **Creating value means solving problems for others**. The world revolves around solving problems. If you aren't solving someone's problem, then you're obsolete. Pharmacists who find themselves let go or downsized are experiencing firsthand what it means to not be valuable to a company. Why should a company maintain your full-time status if it's cheaper for them to hire another part-time pharmacist or a new pharmacy graduate? It isn't ethical, but it's capitalism. **Creating relationships means building genuine friendships, not just networking**. The word "networking" makes me cringe, like watching my younger self in a home video (some are on YouTube for the curious). Networking implies you're looking for something. You naturally know when someone's looking for something from you when they're networking. Managers learn to tune out pharmacists who are looking for jobs. I use the words "create relationships" because you don't need 100 new connections on LinkedIn; they won't get you a job. But what can lead to a new job is a genuine relationship in which you provide value first. We'll dive into the best ways to create value and connection. First, we'll look at relationships, because they are arguably the most important weapon in your indispensable arsenal… and they're probably what you need to work on most. I believe this because you're an intelligent pharmacist—you have innate value—but what you likely lack are the right relationships.

MEET NEW PEOPLE

Your network is your net worth and, like your net worth, the bigger it is, the better off you'll be. Every job I've ever had—even my residency—came to me through someone I knew. So, whether you're looking for opportunities with your current employer, looking for a new pharmacy job, or considering a new career path, you need to start talking! In our social tech world, it isn't difficult to start a conversation with pharmacists all over the world. Maybe you are thinking, "Why would anyone want to meet me? Do I just go an introduce myself? How do I 'break the ice'?" I've found that the easiest way to start a conversation with a stranger you'd like to connect with is to admire their career:

> "Hi Hillary, I'm reaching out to you because I think what you've done with your career is spectacular. You see, I want to do what you do. Just wanted to say that I'd love to meet you and buy you coffee. No worries if you're too busy. Thanks for your time!"

Or,

> "Hi, Joe. I'm connecting with you because I'm looking to get into informatics pharmacy. I found your profile on LinkedIn and thought to myself 'Wow, I'd love to work on the same things as him.' I'd

thought I'd share my admiration and I hope to chat with you someday."

Then, once you have their attention, be sure to do three things:

Listen more than you talk. *Seven Habits of Highly Effective People* by Stephen Covey changed my life, and one of the pieces that resonated most with me was Covey's advice to seek first to understand, then to be understood. He notes that true listening skills are rare: "Most people do not listen with the intent to understand; they listen with the intent to reply." Monitor your next conversation and watch for this habit. How many times do you begin speaking the second the other person has finished? How often do you interrupt others?**Ask questions about what interests others.** Asking questions is the easiest way to get to know someone. Here are some of my go-tos:

- *What do you do?* Icebreakers don't get much easier. This question is a simple way to find out what others do.

- *What's something exciting you're working on?* This is a great question. It sets you up to learn what this person is working on and find a way you might help.

- *If we meet again at next year's conference, what are we celebrating?* I think this is one of the best questions. You'll discover what makes people's hearts move. You find out what makes them tick. It's through this question that you find new opportunities to grow your network, find out what new things people want to accomplish, and how you can help.

Follow up. After you meet someone, follow up with a simple message. A short written note is an easy way for your new contacts to remember you after a conference—but a little creativity can set you apart from the pack. I love using video follow-ups.

I tested out this relationship growth strategy in a relatively pain-free way: Facebook birthday messages. I had a lot of friends on Facebook, but I didn't converse with most of them; it was the perfect testing ground. Getting birthday notifications, even simple ones like "HBD" and "Have a great day," feels good, so I took it a step further and sent a video message to a friend I hadn't been in touch with since pharmacy school. I wished her a happy birthday and probably made a fool of myself telling a bad joke. The next day, I had a response from her: "No one has ever done that for me. It really made my day." From there, it was easy to catch up and breathe life into what had been a cold connection. I kept the experiment going and sent more "happy birthday" video messages and received a similar response almost 100% of the time. In just a few weeks, my Facebook network was a much stronger tool. Now I use video messages as much as possible. After conferences, I spend about an hour going through the business cards I received and sending personalized messages to each. Many times I will record my message using my computer's camera. The idea may scare you, but I've found such a positive response from this. I encourage you to experiment in the way you connect with new people. What do you have to lose, besides hurting the ego?

Your network should be your most significant source of new opportunities. Think of it as another financial asset. Like your 401K, placing consistent deposits into an account will result in a big reward later. Conversely, if you ignore investing in your network, you'll be desperate when you need to use it (i.e., if you lose a job). But it's not just about introductions and growing your lists of second- and third-degree connections—networking the *right* way is about building relationships.

The Wrong Way to Network

Here's a message I received from a "friend" I haven't spoken to in years:

> "Hey, Alex,
>
> I am SO Excited and wanted to let You know that I am launching a NEW company. I think that You will absolutely love it!!
>
> Given [my partners'] 2 Billion Dollar track record, this is going to be massive. And, it's completely different than my previous health company! It's timely, brilliant, innovative, FUN and low maintenance!
>
> Would you like some info on it?"

Yuck. Let's analyze why this message sucks and what you can learn from this failed attempt at relationship-building.

It's impersonal. This is a copied message, likely sent out to her hundreds of contacts on Facebook. Each message you send online should be personalized if you start the conversation. Ideally, you would start a discussion in person, but when that's impossible, email or LinkedIn will have to do. Regardless of the method, you should always provide a personalized approach to each person you contact. **It offers no value**. This network marketer reached out to me because she wants people to join her network and make her more money. She doesn't want to get to know me, my cares, my worries, or my dreams; she's hoping that I am desperate enough for a money-making opportunity. So, to save time, she sent a template message to probe for my desire.

The best way to approach others online is to make your message unique to what the other person cares about. It's clear that this woman did not research me before reaching out. If she had, she would have seen on my Facebook that I'm working on a book and business. She could have asked, "How is your book going?" or "What's new with your business?" Those are things I care about and am happy to discuss. People enjoy sharing and talking about what they love. Don't grow your network to "share an opportunity." Put effort into new relationships because you know a network is worth it.

It's not about me. "I" is our favorite subject. If you noticed, "I" is the most common subject in this networker's message. Her message is more about her than about me.

- "I am so excited…"

- "I am launching…"

- "I think…"

The last thing someone you're reaching out to wants to know is info about you. People only care about what's important to themselves, not what's important to you. Make your messages about the other person. Talk about them. More specifically, talk about how you can help them. You'll never be turned away when you help solve other people's problems. Here lies the problem with most people's networking strategies: The reason most people reach out to others is to solve their own problems (e.g., "I'm reaching out to find a job"). Make your networking all about helping other people. Find out what they want and help them get it.

The Pillar of Smart Relationship-Building

Your message's purpose comes across in all messages you send. Sending an "invitation" like this is a near-guarantee you'll be ignored:

> "Hi Scott, I saw your new job posting at Newberry Hospital. I'm very excited to apply to it. I hoped to speak with you about the new opportunity."

It offers zero value to the reader and instead goes straight to the ask. Why would the recipient feel inclined to respond at all, let alone to set aside time to talk to a stranger who wants something from them? The sad truth is that managers receive these messages all the time and ignore nearly 95% of them. Whenever I coach a new pharmacist, we inevitably have to review how to message brand new people in a network. I have a few modules dedicated to this process in my course Career Jumpstart. The natural urge is to go straight for the ask—but that's like asking to marry someone on the first date. Going for the ask immediately is too big a commitment, and you're likely to be turned down. "Would you marry me?" is a bit much to ask on the first date, so why would you ask a similar question when growing your network?

So how can you help? Can you contribute your expertise? Share an article that calls back to your conversation or connects to what the other person is working on? My favorite approach is to introduce two people who will mutually benefit from knowing one another. Connecting others is an indispensable skill.

Become a "Super-Connector"

Independent pharmacists who want to go in business for themselves occasionally reach out to me for coaching. I enjoy coaching pharmacists in the world on business, but I'd rather connect them with Lester Nathan. Lester is an experienced pharmacy consultant who's helped dozens of pharmacists start up or grow their pharmacies. Better for them to speak with Lester than with me. That introduction was simple, and yet life-changing for the pharmacist. **Who do you know that may be a good fit for a job you heard about? Who in your network could help someone else?** Keep in mind that your network is one of your most valuable career tools, and you should treat it accordingly. Sharing your network connections with others would be the equivalent of a programmer loaning another programmer her computer. In other words, you shouldn't do it for everyone who asks because not everyone deserves access to your friends. Some people are downright crazy. But connecting other like-minded people can be how a new project starts, a future relationship forms, or someone gets a new job. The more you can make these meaningful connections for other people, the more you make yourself indispensable. Imagine the good will you create by spending 10 minutes a week introducing others. Not only would it benefit others, but you feel good, too. Connecting others can be awkward at first. You may not know what to say, or if either party will follow up on your introduction. It's their responsibility to take your introduction to the next step, not yours. I like to highlight the best quality about a person when introducing someone. Honest admiration is a great way to impress on the other person that this introduction is worth their time. Connecting is best done in person, but if that's not possible, then an email will have to do. I'm not a fan of email simply because it's so easy to ignore. Here's an example email I sent introducing two people.

Subject: intro Beau < > Brian

Hi Beau,I mentioned to you my acquaintance Brian. Brian has had success with his business and occasionally helps budding entrepreneurs like you and me. Hi Ben, I mentioned to my friend Beau that you talk with entrepreneurs that do great deals for real estate. Beau is a smart guy and bought some recent sweet deals. I'll let you two set up a call from here!

Brian is a successful pharmacist and entrepreneur who loves helping younger entrepreneurs who need a loan for business growth. He loves being the bank lending out money. When my friend Beau wanted to purchase more rental properties but lacked the funds to do so, introducing him to Brian was a no-brainer. I made the connection, they were able to make a deal that worked for both parties, and all three of us benefited.

Admittedly, this way of giving value first won't happen if your network is dead. A simple way to get started would be to refer your friends to LinkedIn jobs you're not a fit for. As you meet more people, you may be able to connect like-minded people. Justine is a community pharmacist in Florida who thought her social parties were frivolous. She loves getting people together, regardless of the crowd or circumstances. During a coaching session, I discover this to be her zone of genius, the place where she comes alive. We then strategized how she could use this to grow her relationships in the world of pharmacy. Justine became a super-connector by throwing afterhours parties with pharmacists, students, and other local friends. By bringing people together, she discovered new opportunities, namely a few job openings that hadn't been posted online. If you meet someone that you don't believe you can help, find out what their goals are or whom they are hoping to meet. Your network is likely bigger than you think... as long as you take care of it *and* as long as those in your network consider you a meaningful connection. And that brings us to your reputation.

TAKE CARE OF
YOUR REPUTATION

I'm a freak. Yes, I enjoy a hearty helping of Japanese animation about pirates, ninjas, and giant robots. Apparently, my coworkers were well aware of my oddities, which is odd because I'm not the guy at work who raves about his hobbies. At a Christmas party in which we played a game about matching secrets to coworkers, mine was something like, "I watch lots of anime and read manga." Somehow everyone guessed me. I was genuinely surprised since my hobbies are not something I talk about regularly. On the other hand, I'd be shocked if one of my coworkers didn't know that I love speaking in front of crowds. I have a reputation as the guy who enjoys speaking.

What is your reputation at work? Your reputation precedes you everywhere you go: how you treat others, what you're good at, what you're bad at, and where you create value. If you have an excellent reputation and a high endorsement factor (which we'll be discussing later in this chapter), then you're in good shape. If your reputation is lousy—or if you don't have one—then repairing it needs to be at the top of your *Indispensable* to-do list. If you don't restore your reputation, it will follow you into your next interview, a sure-fire way to lower your chances.

What are you known for at your job? Are you known as a complainer? As someone who throws a fuss whenever there's a new task? As the pharmacist who messes up the store? As the pharmacist who doesn't get along with the technicians? Who are you to other people? What do they think of you?

Everyone has different strengths to be used in different situations. How can you use your unique ability to build a reputation that receives more of the work you enjoy? Go do that thing.

As your reputation grows, you'll find that people turn to you to help them. This effect won't happen overnight; it is a long-term strategy, much like many of my suggestions, for creating a lasting change. The ideal shift is that people come to you for opportunities. You become the picky hustler rather than the desperate beggar.

What Do You Want to be Known For?

Ash, a Canadian pharmacist, began working with me to improve his retail career. He worked in the typical large chain setting and wanted freedom from the monotony. He didn't know his unique ability or where he wanted to work, only that he wanted out. We sussed out his unique ability through our coaching conversations. Ash shared numerous times that he enjoyed projects in the past where he had to analyze data points. When conversing with pharmacists at this stage of the career jumpstart, I find that once a pharmacist brings up a certain kind of work three times, that's a sign.

Ash spent the next two months connecting with pharmacists in analytical positions and working on a pharmacy service economic analysis for publication. His unique analytical ability became the focal point of his conversations. Old acquaintances he reached out to were introducing him to new people about his analysis project. Soon he became known among circles in Ottawa as the "guy with the research project." Ash was steps ahead of his competition by landing interviews for these analytical management jobs.

You can change what you are known for. Once you understand your unique ability, you can flex those muscles. Your network will grow as you talk with others about your ability or what your ability leads you to work on.

Your unique ability goes hand in hand with your reputation. Begin to work in your newfound unique ability, and you'll find new opportunities to practice and likely new colleagues.

Up Your Endorsement Factor

A movie's rating can't change easily. When *Star Wars: The Last Jedi* came out, some critics loved it, but according to Rotten Tomatoes, the audience didn't. Their bad reviews influenced the movie's sales. Despite what critics might say, it's the audience's reception that shapes others' opinions and determines a movie's success.

In the same way, your network's opinion of you will influence your career's success (or lack thereof). The good news is that, unlike a low-rated movie, you can change things about you that make you more endorsable—but it will probably require some change on your part. You need to build up people's trust in you.

For every movie I'm interested in seeing, I will watch my favorite movie-reviewing YouTuber, Chris Stuckmann, before committing time to the movie. Over the years, he's built my trust of his movie reviews, and I almost always agree with his assessments and insights into the film. I don't look for other reviewers' opinions because I trust Chris. Obviously, I would endorse him to anyone looking for a good movie reviewer.

You can improve your endorsement factor. As you work on the things that make you recommendable, you will find people referring you to jobs. You won't have to search for jobs on Indeed. But to get referred for jobs, you need to have trust, which is earned and never given. **Trust is your career's most valuable asset. Without it, why would anyone put their own reputation on the line to help you?** Building trust takes time, of course. As you perform tasks and projects and meet (or miss) your commitments, other people will decide on whether they can depend on you. Here are three habits you can improve to increase their confidence and up your endorsement factor.

Show Up on Time

Do you have a tech or pharmacist on your team who *almost always* doesn't show up on time? What's your impression of that person? Is that someone you could trust to open a pharmacy? Is that someone who you would trust to give a project to with a definite deadline? Probably not.

It's our natural response not to trust people who don't show up on time. By not showing up on time, you send a message to others. "You're not important enough for my attention." When another person makes an effort to be on time and ready, you disrespect their efforts by being late. Imagine if everyone treated each other's time with respect. No meeting would run late or start late. It would take no extra time from you. If you're late to the trivial matter of a meeting or work, then how could you expect someone to refer you to another job? Can you imagine a past boss saying, "She was always late for work, but I would definitely recommend her."

Of course, there are reasonable explanations for why you don't show up on time. But when they happen more than once, you show your true colors. The way to change this habit is to notice where you are deficient first. Plan accordingly. I had a colleague who showed up late every day to work. His explanations in the past have been poor sleep, lack of sleep, and distractions at home, and other random excuses.

Being late to work consistently shouldn't be a surprise to you and give you the excuse to rely on. Your work schedule shouldn't be a surprise to you. It's like the chronically late person thinks, "Oh, I can't believe work starts at eight again today." They've always known when work starts, but they follow other priorities that make them late.

Plan your day ahead of time. If you have a chronic excuse for being late, expect that excuse to happen again and plan it into your day. For example, I plan for every weekday that my children will distract me from 7:00 to 7:40 am, right before I go to work. My kids can cause me to lose track of time spent with them (usually because I'm having fun), and I'll walk out the door ten minutes late. But I schedule wiggle room every morning to be with them, it gives me enough time to plan for distractions as I'm getting ready for work.

Do What You Say

I had a friend in college who I loved being around. He and I had tons of fun together. We spent many nights playing group games like Rock Band and watched classic movies. But eventually, I broke ties with him. The effort on my part wore on me. You see, my friend had a habit of promising to hang out, but would then bail on me 90% of the time. I tired of this habit and stopped inviting him over.

One day my friend asked me about why I stopped asking to hang out. I told him the truth, "You hardly show up." What I was saying was, "I can't trust you to do what you say." People like this don't make it far in careers. Only people who follow through on their promises can build trust.

This has been a difficult habit for me to master. I grew a habit from a young age to promise things with lip service, but never follow through. In my short career, I've learned to discipline myself to do what I say. The best tactic to improve this is by holding myself accountable to others and creating a realistic action plan. And of course, I always use my Google calendar for reminders.

Finish What You Start

A half-done project is as worthless as a 95% completed project. Always finish what you start.

During my entrepreneur journey, I told myself I would do multiple projects, but more often than not I would fail to complete them. I started blog posts that I never published. I wrote a few non-fiction books that went nowhere.

Procrastination is an epidemic in the modern world, especially for our perfectionistic pharmacy culture. We escalate simple tasks into big, unsolvable problems (like a career transition), and that leads us to hold off on making any significant change. Take one small step at a time if you feel overwhelmed. Those who don't finish what they start create a reputation of avoidance. No one wants to give that person a project because they think, "He'll never finish it and then I'll have more work to do."

Also, know when to say "no." As you explore your zone of genius, you'll find more opportunities to explore. Perhaps too many options will appear. You do not want to over-extend yourself because your output won't be 100%. Projects will slip through the cracks, deadlines will be missed, and you may slip into the zone of excellence or competence instead of the zone of genius.

Say Please and Thank You

Polite people get what they want. To be polite means to be respectful of others without aggressiveness. Polite people get referred. The opposite, rudeness or even a lack of niceties, will not advance your career. This habit should be ubiquitous throughout your workday.

Hopefully, your parent instilled in you "please" and "thank you." As a parent of two young girls, I am reminded throughout the day how little I say please and thank you. I probably say it as often as my colleagues, but I haven't been the leader.

Here's a simple test for you to do: visit a competitor's pharmacy (or another similar workplace) and listen to interactions. Go undercover if you have to. Buy a trench coat and a shady hat. How many pleases and thank yous did you count? I visited a local grocery store to test my experiment. I counted three pleases and five thank yous in a ten-minute period.

Finally, you've got to create value to become an indispensable pharmacist with a high endorsement factor. That one is so important it gets its own chapter.

CREATE VALUE

The marketplace for pharmacists depends on value. A valuable pharmacist has unique skills. A low-value pharmacist is someone who is easily replaceable. I know there are exceptions to the rule, but in general, a part-time retail pharmacist isn't hard to find. "Anyone can do the job," as one manager put it. That means the job and skills required aren't valuable. There's little value to be created. This pharmacist can follow the standard rules, achieve goals, and maybe be seen as a go-getter, and that could lead to future promotions if desired within the company. But is she indispensable? Are you?

What value do you currently bring to your job?

My fourth year of pharmacy school caused great anxiety. I realized that I wanted to commit fully to the residency track, but my last three years of school had little to show for accomplishments, other than surviving classes. My CV was relatively empty. I knew that my competition would blow me away. I went into emergency career-building mode. I applied for every volunteer opportunity. Anything that would look decent on my CV, even if it wasn't directly related to my career focus.

Ultimately, my efforts didn't show for much. They did little to convince residency program directors I was worth asking for an interview. I only received one interview request out of nine applications! I learned a valuable lesson too late: employers look at your track record of creating value to gauge what you could bring to their company.

The best (and easiest) way to increase *your* value immediately is by creating additional value at your current job or activities. Let's talk about some of the easiest ways you can create value tomorrow at your job.

Make Someone Smile

If you have the pleasure of one day visiting the Grandville, Michigan, Meijer superstore, you may run into Gregory Baily. Meijer is a superstore competitor to the likes of Walmart and may have them running hard for their money. Gregory captured my attention my first visit to Meijer during my third year of pharmacy school. My fellow Class of 2012 Ferris Bulldogs may know who I'm talking about.

As I entered the store, I distinctly remember the man dressed as a Meijer greeter said: "Feeling groovy?" and I replied with a shocked smile, "You bet, man!" I remember that making me laugh and just making me feel good.

I'm not the only person whose day improved because of Greg. He's so popular that he's received awards and mentions in the local news. I learned of Meijer fans that would travel further distances just to meet Greg. His bosses would have to be stupid to ever risk losing him. As Greg Baily shows, the easiest way to create value in someone's day is a smile. Being weird is my favorite way to cause a smile.

I don't hide that I'm a nerd. I love *Star Wars*. I love Japanese anime. There's a soft spot in my heart for the *Lord of the Rings*—heck, I shed a few tears after my first viewing. And that makes me a person. Being weird is being human. Unfortunately, too many pharmacists are unwilling to be human during the entire job search process. Professionalism has beaten personality out of pharmacy. Everyone is stiff and scared out of their minds, which makes it impossible for them to show up as the humans they are. Justine, a pharmacist I worked with, had an awkward interview process for one of her jobs. She had to do a recorded interview, in which she had to film herself on the computer answering a few questions. Naturally, she was nervous about the situation.

After I helped her overcome the fear of recording herself, we discussed prepping for the interview. She asked me, "How can I force myself to be normal when it's so weird recording myself?" I thought for a moment and said, "Well, why not point that out during the interview and make a joke about it?"

So she did. Justine opened her recording with, "Have you ever sang to yourself in the mirror? You're thinking that no one is watching, but you find out that someone is, but more than someone, your boss is watching. That's what this interview feels like."

She later found out that this moment of humanity was the main reason she was invited to do a second interview (in a field in which she had no experience in, I might add). The hiring manager said, "You were surprisingly natural, and I can find no one who seems so calm during the interview process."

Give (Sincere) Compliments

I love giving compliments... but I love receiving them more. I have to admit: nothing feels better than when someone notices something about me.

Now, I'm a hard six on the "looks scale." Maybe a seven if I'm wearing something slick. (My wife says I'm a ten, but you know that love is blind.) So if someone compliments me on my attire or looks, my ego gets a boost and I feel better about myself. I won't lie, it doesn't take much for me to feel good from a compliment—and that makes *sincere* compliments a fantastic value-creating tool. Don't see this tactic as sleazy, unless you plan on not giving sincere compliments. The world doesn't need another liar. It needs your honest admiration. As an old pharmacy mentor told me once, "Treat everyone like they're your future boss."

When reaching out to grow your relationships, simply provide a compliment to someone without expecting anything in return. Everyone on LinkedIn is looking for something (a new job mainly), but a compliment is never expected. Giving one may be the best way to create quick value in a new relationship.

How to Create the Most Value? Get Inside Their Head

You spent three to four years in pharmacy school to learn everything to prepare for the NAPLEX, a test that determines whether or not you are competent enough to do the job. Once passed, you forget 90% of everything that was on the test, and then you practice pharmacy, only to find out that the vast majority of what you do is negated by patient psychology.

Medication adherence rates in the USA are abysmal. Even I can't remember to give my kid every dose of her amoxicillin. Doing pharmacy is hardly just therapeutics. We interact with complex human beings with a vast array of emotions and motivators. Once you begin working, you quickly learn that people won't do what you tell them to do. In recent years, one of the more prominent solutions to this problem is motivational interviewing, which the typical community pharmacist has no time for implementing. Motivational interviewing is perhaps one of the most important skills you can learn as a pharmacist. Essentially, the skill helps you and a patient determine what's important to the patient and motivate them to take a medication.

Outside of healthcare, this skill is known as selling, and unfortunately, selling, marketing, or branding is rarely taught in pharmacy school, or even as an MBA.

Branding yourself in the job market is essential for the indispensable pharmacist. You have to stand out when your competition is going for the same job. The best way to stand out is to understand what your future boss is thinking. If you understand their thoughts about a potential job, then you can speak to their needs and present yourself as the best solution.

I've written before that pharmacists don't know how to sell themselves. Here's the simple step to get started: Think like your future boss.

Think Like a Manager

Frank Abagnale Jr. successfully forged checks for millions of dollars before his 19th birthday. This was just the start of his career as a con artist. Frank also practiced medicine without a license, flew planes without a license, and practiced law without a license. He fooled everyone, including himself at points in his life.

The law followed him everywhere. FBI agents pursued him to bring him in, but Frank had a knack for escape plans. *Catch Me If You Can,* the movie based on Frank's life, features a great scene where Frank, played by Leonardo DiCaprio, meets with an FBI agent, played by Tom Hanks. Frank fools the FBI agent into believing Frank is not Frank Abagnale Jr. but another FBI agent who's already captured the real Frank Abagnale Jr. The scene has you screaming, "That's the real Frank!" Or, if you're rooting for Frank, "Run!"

Catch Me If You Can is a great story about influence. Frank Abagnale Jr. lived his life using influence to meet his desires. He knew what others thought, and so he played to those beliefs to fool people, which highlights a valuable lesson about influence: to influence someone, you must think like them. So to think like a manager (particularly your future boss), you have to ponder these questions:

- What do I want for my employees?

- How can I help them succeed?

- What are the outcomes I care about?

- What will make me look good?

As you consider your answers, you'll unearth a plethora of new opportunities for creating value.

What Do I Want for My Employees?

You may have rotten feelings toward your current manager, or you may believe your boss is a regular Mother Teresa. Regardless of your feelings, your manager wants something from you.

- Make me look good (ego)

- Earn me more money (wealth)

- Build my business (opportunity)

- Obey my commands (ego)

- Grow to your potential (love)

A manager wants to work with an employee who is likable, competent, and will fit into the company's work culture.

Think of your current (or last) boss. To understand her/his desires, let's ask a few questions. What was her main work priority for you? What were you constantly asked to do? What came up in your annual review? What opportunities did he present to you?

While you may begin to feel negative emotions toward your manager, I urge you to look past their flaws and focus on what they focused on with you. Your answers will potentially highlight a new accomplishment for you to add to your value-creating resume.

What Outcomes Do I Care About?

Your manager likely has more stress than you realize. Not only does she deal with you, but likely dozen(s) of other employees, some more troublesome. She doesn't have time to address all your concerns or even spend time to help you develop your career. The best way to maximize your current job's value is by aligning your unique ability with your company's objective.

Here's a common problem many pharmacists run into when growing their unique ability. Once a pharmacist understands what they are great at, they want to find opportunities. As they look at their options at work, they become discouraged. They think, "There's no way my boss would let me do this." They may give up, never ask the boss, or simply dismiss the idea. The problem is simple: the belief there are no options at the current job to grow a unique ability.

You may find opportunities for deploying your unique ability at work. Check your company's last newsletter. Read your boss's emails. Find out what company events they're praising, like immunization or health clinics. Read past emails about things other pharmacists are doing that intrigue you. Find out how you could become involved. Ask yourself, where can I apply my unique ability at work?

What Will Make Me Look Good?

Don't underestimate someone's ego. Everyone loves praise. Managers look good to their superiors when their team is doing good. No manager wants their team to fail; ultimately it looks poor to their supervisor. Supervisors may not like your plan for change. One pharmacist discovered she loved working her hands, so she wished to pursue compounding. There was one compounding pharmacy in their division. She shared her fears about asking her manager: "He'll probably say no or ask why I'm looking for a change." Not every manager will be supportive of your career intentions. Some may block you from volunteering for certain projects. If you try, and can't figure out how to make this a win-win situation, you may find luck helping outside your company. However, don't let your pessimism dissuade you from asking. Performing with your unique ability should make your manager look good. As you flex your ability, you should ultimately perform at a higher level and create a unique accomplishment. A pharmacist I helped named Hank found he enjoyed working in his retail store's clinics, but was rarely asked to be involved. After speaking with the clinical pharmacy coordinator at headquarters, Hank learned from her that she found it difficult to get pharmacists to volunteer for clinics. He soon found himself getting paid to do more of what he loved. After a few clinics, his manager commended his performance because of the increase in immunizations as well as an increase in medical device sales, all accomplishments that made Hank's resume look more attractive to new employers.

Anticipate Needs

My beloved college car had to be given up. My wife and I co-decided the car was an unnecessary expense during my residency. We wanted to live as frugally as possible, so we became a one-car family, with a baby on the way. After receiving my real first pharmacy job, we decided we needed two cars. My wife loves to research online. She's like a deal-hunting Indiana Jones. She had an idea of what kind of car she wanted (the new car would be hers to use mainly). We traveled to a local car dealership to experience one of the worst car salesmen I have ever dealt with.

Soon after entering, he was on us like a hawk on a baby rabbit. Megan told him what we were looking for (a small mini-van) and our price range. He listened, and didn't hear us. Because what he brought out were vehicles we didn't want. He brought out sedans, coupes, and other used cars we didn't like or want. We left the dealership shortly after he showed us the third option. The car salesman is guilty of the most important selling sin: He didn't understand our needs.

Let's contrast his story with the second car salesman, who we ultimately bought from.

The second car dealership had a more modern feeling immediately entering the facility. We were greeted by a receptionist who offered us coffee (always welcome, especially during the winter snow) and said that a specialist would be right out to help us. A specialist? As I remember our first experience, I looked to my wife and sarcastically said, "Must be smart," hoping I would get a slap on the arm. Megan ignored my lame dad humor.

We were directed to the specialist's office and he performed a thorough questionnaire about what we wanted, what we were looking for, and want we wanted to avoid. He listened. At the end of the day, we drove home as happy new owners of a Mazda Sudan. Car enthusiasts may be cringing, but we were happy, particularly my wife.

The second car salesman anticipated our needs. Even though he asked us questions, after our experience I reflected on how he guided us to our decision. He knew our needs and "helped" us avoid poorer car options.

Over my years as an entrepreneur, I had to learn from the school of hard knocks about selling. I made enough mistakes, but I learned from great salesmen, too. One of the concepts I adopted on early was to "Anticipate the customer's needs." Knowing what your customer needs before they ask for it will increase the likelihood of a purchase. The same is true in your career.

Your resume, cover letter, and LinkedIn account are a reflection of your brand. A brand is a representation of what an entity can sell. Most career brands are pretty boring, if not repetitive of everyone else.

How to Get Into A Hiring Manager's Head

Anticipate your future boss's needs with your *Indispensable* brand and you'll make your career search easier. How can you know your future boss' needs? The simplest way would be to talk to her or him, but perhaps the easier way is to look at the job description from either the company's website or a job board.

A job description provides (usually) a poor description of what the company expects the employee to do. Luckily these descriptions often report what experience they're looking for, particularly regarding personal qualities.

To sell your brand to your future boss, you must know what's important to him or her. The best question to ask yourself to know this is: What would your future boss want to see in your cover letter, resume, CV, application, or interview? Some of this is on the job description. You can take their qualities, skills, or accomplishments as sales copy (a term to designate words used for selling). Your entire application is your ability to sell yourself. The job description can guide what you should do next in your career development. Take one quality or experience required in the position and ask yourself, "What would it take to show to my future boss that I'm excellent at [insert quality]?"

I call this process "job reverse engineering." The only way to make a job transition is by showing your future boss you have the potential. Hiring managers have been taught for decades that the best predictor of success in a new job is to look at past successes and failures. This is why you hand in a resume. They want to know your past performance to predict your future performance at the company.

There are a plethora of qualities and experience options to choose on a job description. How do you know which ones to focus on? Ideally, you'll be able to pick up which skills are the most important, but if you don't know which, the best thing would be to ask a few people already in the industry. Through your networking, you should already know a few people who could provide their insider knowledge. Preferably, you should ask a manager what matters most.

Be a Giver

My childhood shaped my "taker" adulthood. I'm an only child, as many of my friends like to point out, saying, "Alex, you only think about yourself." I didn't have to share with others, which created a self-focused mentality. What I craved most as a child was attention. Not attention from adults, but from other kids. My greatest joy was being the center of attention in all environments. The classroom, gym lunchroom, Sunday school, I sought after the attention of others, even at the expense of others.

I quickly learned that I could make other people laugh. I took every moment to tell a joke, to be silly, to turn attention my way. Of course, this attention didn't come without consequences. I had more detentions than all my classmates combined because of my reckless (and obnoxious) behavior. In my webinars, I like to show an old detention slip that reads, "Alex said 'screw you' after I asked him to figure something out by himself." Yeah, it's not my proudest moment, but it highlights a philosophy I grew into: *What can I get out of you?*

This was an underlying thought in all my interactions:

> *How can I get everyone in this room to laugh?*
>
> *What can I do to get people to notice me?*
>
> *How can I befriend this person?*
>
> *How can he make my life easier?*
>
> *What can she do in our class group so I don't have to do as much work?*
>
> *How can I do the least amount of work possible?*
>
> *What can I say to make this person think the best of me?*
>
> *How can I use this relationship for my betterment?*

I took what I wanted without giving something in exchange. I was what Adam Grant calls a "taker." Grant's book, *Give and Take*, defines people as either a giver, someone who gives without expecting anything in return, or a taker, who tries to get something to serve their desires while guarding their expertise and time. I fell into the takers camp. Do you?

> When is the last time you gave into someone else's career?
>
> When is the last time you referred someone else to a job?

When is the last time you introduced someone to a manager who had a job?

If you're like me, these questions will strike a chord. And, if you're like me, you're probably looking for ways to become a giver.

What Giving First Does to Your Career

Marissa is a community pharmacist at a busy store. She has more responsibilities than she can handle. It wouldn't surprise you to know she is consistently behind and feels like she can never catch up. One of her tasks is preceptorship, and it often turns into the lowest priority.

Students have a talent for making your day-to-day job even more stressful. Maybe they suck at personal skills, and you cringe at all their patient interactions. You don't have the time to manage them, let alone make them into a great pharmacist. Marissa can relate.

But Marissa decided one day to help these struggling students. Each student she enjoyed became a potential candidate for employment at her company. She spent time with students and often used their time to be her "technicians" because corporate removed her full-time technician. She recruited fifteen pharmacists over six years.

Her work in recruitment (a volunteer responsibility she took on) led her to become the go-to person for on-site training. This is responsibility she at first refused (because who has time to help others?), but reluctantly accepted.

After talking with Marissa, she never thought about how this was a valuable asset to any company. Do you know how much it costs to recruit a pharmacist? Depending on the job and location, recruitment can cost a company anywhere from a few thousand dollars to well over $40,000 (think winter in Alaska). She likely saved her company over $100,000 in expenses.

Marissa just created value without realizing it. She wasn't hired to do recruitment. But instead of the company having a "loss" of $100,000, Marissa created the unique value of fifteen new pharmacist jobs.

When I first reviewed Marissa's resume, it had all the typical mistakes: broad generalizations about her skills, a lack of accomplishments, and an overall lackluster description of her actual abilities. After asking questions, I found out about her recruitment of fifteen pharmacists and asked her, "Why did you not include this on your resume?" Her response shocked me: "This is a normal duty I have, so I didn't think to include it."

Any value you create at your job should be on your resume. Marissa's accomplishment became one of her top bullet points and became a consistent point of discussion during interviews. Giving first in your career looks like Marissa's story. Giving first involves finding a need for your company and meeting it. No one else volunteered to recruit new pharmacists. Marissa took the initiative and solved a problem. Her work created trust with her manager, which is career gold.

Marissa's drive led her to become the number one pharmacist in her district (another accomplishment that wasn't on her resume) even though she "hated" her job. Her action of giving first created many discussions with hiring managers, recruiters, and fellow pharmacists. Giving first ups your endorsement factor. People want to share how awesome and indispensable you are.

GO BEYOND THE MANAGER

"Alex, does ranitidine make you constipated?"

You probably get all sorts of medical questions, especially from your family. My mom loves to ask me medication questions. She values my knowledge, and in a pinch it's saved her some trouble. While mommy values my knowledge, the same isn't true about the public.

Society at large, in my opinion, doesn't value pharmacy. Here is why: we are a free service. The public only has to wait to speak with a pharmacist to access them. This isn't true for doctors. Imagine if doctors were as accessible as pharmacists. Those doctors who are readily accessible to the public are those in emergency rooms or telehealth services, all of which accrue a cost.

Imagine if your grandma received an insurance bill called a "pharmacist consultation" the next time she asked a pharmacist a question. You'd hear about it right? Well, if the public doesn't value pharmacy, who do they value? Experts.

Experts are asked to interviews, consulted, sought after. Experts are given important projects. Experts are given more responsibility and more ways to show they are valuable. Experts receive opportunities.

An expert commands job market attention. Experts don't need to worry about where their next opportunity will come from. Companies view their knowledge and experience as worth the price.

With today's avenues, it's possible to turn yourself into an expert.

BECOME AN EXPERT

After you discovered your ikigai, unique ability, and zone of genius, you can pinpoint a career path for yourself. After identifying your path, find an established expert within the field. Your goal is to become like this person. Do the valuable things she/he is doing, and you won't fail to create an indispensable career.

Let's show you how anyone can become an expert, step by step.

Jeremy was a community chain pharmacist. Hated his job. Didn't think his job would lead to any fulfillment. Family life became rough over the years. His marriage was stressed. He felt like he was failing his kids by not being there for them. This was a typical starting point for most clawing their way out of a dispensable career hole.

Jeremy and I discovered his unique ability: empathetic communication. He enjoys breaking down complex ideas into easy-to-understand key points, but only when they matter to the patient. He found great dissatisfaction in his work because the company's priority was the exact opposite of what he desires to do with patients. The company was more concerned about number care than health care.

After digging deep with Jeremy, we found his zone of genius. Jeremy comes alive when he is listening to and teaching those in great physical pain. He finds himself moved by their emotions. That feeling makes him into his best self. Helping these patients brought the best out of him. What he produces then becomes his greatest output.

Next we found Jeremy's curiosity again. After being stuck for about four years, the job drained his curiosity. He didn't know where to start. To discover his curiosity, I encouraged him to do something he's never done before, but had always been interested in doing. His answer: smoke a joint. All right, man. While I encourage curiosity, I also want people to obey the law. He agreed to speak with a friend who could speak to his curiosity about pain relief and marijuana.

A week later I asked Jeremy, "Find a supplier yet?" He declined, but replied with what he learned about marijuana medical applications.

Something sparked within Jeremy. His curiosity flourished in this moment. He wasn't absorbed by despair. He became obsessed by the possibilities of marijuana and pain relief. After talking with patients who used marijuana, he found himself empowered to pursue a new pharmacy career path. So, what did he do next to stand out from his competition?

He devoured content on marijuana and pharmacy. Over the period of a month, he knew every recent marijuana study or discovery. He could tell me where the industry was and what problems it faced. He created lists of every legal dispensary within 50 miles of him. He found himself wanting to share his new-found-knowledge with friends and family. Jeremy previously shared during a chat his enjoyment of writing, so I encouraged him to write about this journey online. He did. By sharing his knowledge online, the public views him as an expert. Why? Because you only need to know a little bit about something to know more than 95% of the general public. He delivered continuing education, at first not about marijuana, but about pain relief, and where marijuana could fit into the bigger picture. He spoke to any audience willing to learn, which included nurse practitioners, physicians, and occupational and physical therapists. These CE events garnered attention from medical cannabis dispensary owners. He created relationships with each owner, and picked the owner he liked the most. He approached the owner with a job pitch, a description of the job Jeremy wanted to do most. The owner saw the value immediately (because much of the pitch was about how Jeremy would solve the problems the owner faced) and invited him to the nicest steak restaurant in town.

The dinner was an impromptu meeting about the owner. At the end, the owner offered Jeremy a job. When Jeremy asked the owner why he choose him over other pharmacists, he replied, "You know more about our industry than I do!"

Value is perceived by the beholder. When aiming for a new job, your best strategy is to create your own expertise.

NO ONE WILL GIVE ME A CHANCE

How do I create value or become an expert when no one gives me a chance?

Creating value is one of the best strategies I recommend pharmacists do to help them transition into a new career. I get the above question a lot about the "how" part.

We don't live in a permission society anymore. No one needs to permit you positively contributing to a company. Creating value means a track record of helping someone else with their goals. That could be:

- writing a grant proposal

- teaching a free class

- leading a free clinic

- volunteering in a workgroup (association or government)

- or simply sharing your thoughts in a blog

Write a blog post on LinkedIn. It's free. Share it with others. There are so many friends I have on LinkedIn whose lives are centered around their blogs. For some, it's practically their job now, or how they got a new job.

Don't know what to say? Talk about solutions to problems that companies have.

I told myself years ago, "No one will listen to you or read your blog." Now my blog gets 10K monthly visitors and supplies my family's needs. Your commitment to changing your career trajectory could lead you to become a thought leader in your desired niche. No one is stopping you from contributing online.

You don't need a solid gold idea to create value for a company. You need to discover the problems you care about, and either volunteer or create a solution. Do this over time, and it'll lead to new opportunities.

Well, What About...

A common roadblock people stumble onto sounds like this, "How can I create expertise in something I don't get to practice? There's no way a hospital will hire a community pharmacist because a community pharmacist has no expertise or practical experience. I can't write a blog and get out of retail and into another job."

First I'll say: not true. We've worked with community pharmacists who transition into hospital. They don't get ICU cardiology specialist jobs, but they start off as a staff or even outpatient pharmacist.

So, how does a busy pharmacist become an expert on a subject, especially if she doesn't know how to develop a skill she can't find a way to practice?

- Set your goal

- Identify the subject

- Study

- Apply

- Teach

- Lead

One of my favorite examples on this was an old mentor's career story. Don was a typical staff pharmacist in the 1970s. Nothing special about the beginning of his career. One day, he had a patient develop an allergic reaction to Penicillin. He found himself on the floor with the patient and the doctor. The doctor asked Don to find some new therapy choices. Don couldn't come up with a great option on the spot, but the request sparked a curiosity that wasn't there before. Later, Don **identified his goal:** learn more about infectious disease. Over the next ten years Don developed his expertise. He **studied** at work and home. He **applied** his knowledge by **teaching** presentations on new antibiotics, by developing policies and guidelines, consulting physicians and leading the hospital's infectious disease team. Don developed a reputation at the hospital: the go-to-guy for infectious disease treatments. Don eventually transitioned into a full-time position doing infectious disease.

You could say Don was lucky, that those opportunities don't happen now. You need a residency to qualify for those jobs. Well, then start where you can and work your way to your goal. You don't need to leap into your next job. You just need to take the next small step forward.

You could publish your thoughts on LinkedIn, which has a free blog platform (at the time of this writing). You could volunteer to write for your state's pharmacy association, or local medical group, or a hospital. You could volunteer to teach a CE for multiple professions (and be paid to do so). You could create a YouTube video or a podcast (if you think you have a face for radio, like I do).

Teaching others is how I got to where I am today. I'm not smarter than you. You are capable of increasing your curious knowledge and sharing it with others. That's how to become an expert.

SHOULD I START A BUSINESS?

As you read this book, you may find yourself asking, "Should I start a business?" While the business path was a part of my journey, it may or may not be yours. It certainly doesn't hurt to have something on the side making income. But the journey isn't for everyone.

In my humble opinion, I believe being in business for yourself is the safest career move.

What happens if your one source of income disappears?

You'll need to collect unemployment until you find another job, right? Unemployment has plenty of requirements, such as applying to jobs on a regular basis. It doesn't have to be a pharmacist job, mind you. It needs to be any job. In the current market, more and more pharmacists have to apply to jobs outside pharmacy when on unemployment. You begin to rely on savings, and you feel the money noose tightening around your neck. Perhaps your partner is berating you, "Just find something!" or "I don't understand why you can't find something. You're a doctor for crying out loud." You're darn tooting you are. That doesn't change the fact our job market is saturated. The easy jobs are taken quickly, or given to new grads who will take less money.

Renay was a fifty-something pharmacist in the saturated market of St. Louis, Missouri. She lost her job in January 2018, which was a short-term contract hospital job. Unfortunately the contracts stopped coming. Every week she applied to 5 to 10 jobs, whether or not they were in pharmacy.

Her sole income vanished, leaving her to fend for herself. Now, what would happen if Renay had a part-time business?

Let's say one client left Renay. Well, she could always find another client. But it wouldn't be the end of the business. She would have other clients to serve and in turn she would be paid by multiple clients. A business allows you to find multiple streams of income, rather than rely on one like a job.

My first job supplied the majority of my income, but I wanted to transition into a "lifestyle" business, which relies on multiple streams of income. Now I live off my business, which has dozens of people contributing over time. People will not always want to do business with me, and some people demand refunds, a normal part of business life. But if one person, or even ten people, demand a refund, I won't be worried about lost income. I have plenty left over, or, if I was really hurting, I could hustle for a while and find more clients.

Safe is relative. In my view, having one job, one sole income stream, is extremely risky compared to running a business.

All it takes is one person to not like you, and you could be back on the streets, looking for your next job, wondering who will take you in, potentially uprooting your whole family just to find employment.

I'll be brief to explain the how part because this subject easily could become a new book. Here's the step-by-step approach:

- Find a need

- Provide a service/product for freeValidate the need for the service/productGather testimonials from happy clients

- Set up shop and start charging

This summary is so short that I feel like I'm committing a crime. Discovering if business is for you is a self-development process that challenges your core beliefs, what you really want from life, and what you value most. Rather than dive deeper here, I'll recommend you check out my class Side Hustle Fast Track for Pharmacists: *https://happy-pharmd.teachable.com/p/side-hustle-fast-track-for-pharmacists*. I have three modules (with over 30 total lessons) on the three phases of building a business fast:

- Module 1: Create your idea

- Module 2: Validate your idea

- Module 3: Scale your idea

I've taught this material to over 500 pharmacists. Some have successful side hustles that create an extra $1,000 a month, while others have turned the lessons into full-time jobs. But for every success story, there are failures. Not everyone is cut out for business, but it could be the next stage of your career that leads to a job.

Business isn't without its own risks and negative aspects. But know this, my friend: you can choose a career path that makes you happy and indispensable.

CONCLUSION

When I moved back to my hometown, I didn't like it. The population sits at around 3,000 (mostly old) folks. We have one streetlight, a McDonald's, a grocery store, and a depressing downtown area. I hated that I was back home. I had told everyone in high school that I would move away and live somewhere exciting. Nashville, maybe Denver or Dallas or San Diego… that's where I belonged. I never dreamed of small city life! I loved living in Grand Rapids during my grad school years at Ferris State. And then there I was: taking my first official "adult" job in my hometown. I couldn't believe it, and deep down I hated myself. I felt like I was "better" than everyone else in the area and stuck my nose up at our nearby restaurants, concerts in the park, and events. I rejected the idea that I belonged here. I convinced myself I still felt the call of the city.

Those feelings soon bled into my work life, and I practiced pharmacy with that same chip on my shoulder. Workdays turned sour as I dealt with bullies, a difficult manager, and an unwelcome change in my position. I felt like I had been lied to, that the whole profession was a lie. I had busted my butt for seven years to earn this pharmacy degree, only to find that I hated the work. It all seemed like a waste of my life. As my mindset spiraled, I rejected my identity as a pharmacist and took on a new identity as an entrepreneur.

Being an entrepreneur was so much more fun, though I never committed to one idea long enough to make it work out. I'd bounce from idea to idea, throw myself into the work until, oh, about the six-month mark. Then I would question my idea, my "lack of results," my business, and eventually, I would give up. All this time I had nagging thoughts like, "Why not build a business in pharmacy? You have all this experience; you should use it." But the chip on my shoulder wouldn't let go. "I can't stay in pharmacy!" I thought. "It's the exact opposite direction I want in my life." If I returned to the profession, I would be a hypocrite. I couldn't do it. I *wouldn't* do it. But my entrepreneur journey wasn't leading me to the freedom I desired. I couldn't commit to one business idea long enough to see real success. Fear crept in as I compared my results to others who were more successful than myself, which was the worst thing I could have done. You can't compare your start to someone else's finish line. My fear told me to try something different, and I listened. I ran away as soon as the journey got too difficult and started yet another new entrepreneurial endeavor: a "media" company. I created pharmacy media, including articles, videos, and audio, for companies who paid me a hefty amount for my work. The company's early success and all the money it brought in felt like a slap in the face: "Wake up, Alex. Your ego is in the way. Pharmacy is your expertise, teaching and writing is your unique ability, and you can get paid well for it." Ego is a funny thing. It holds us back from making the decisions that, though humbling, lead to a freer lifestyle. This time, I pushed past my ego and moved into the pharmacy space, but still, my fear came with me.

It wasn't until I met with my mastermind group in December 2016 that I spoke about the fear that had been following me: "I feel like I should be further in my entrepreneur journey than where I am today." I recognized that changing my entrepreneurial direction hindered my efforts, but I was terrified of the success I might achieve. My mastermind group called me out on my lack of commitment. They challenged me to commit to something for longer than six months. After the call, I sat in silence. I sensed the weight of the decision before me. "What will you do, Alex?"

Can You Commit?

I took two weeks to decide, but at our next meeting, I reported to my mastermind group: "I will commit to The Happy PharmD for 18 months. If I can't reach the success goals I set for myself by then, then I will quit and pursue another project."

It was a landmark decision for me and one of the best things I've ever done for myself. Within six months of committing to The Happy PharmD "business," I replicated my monthly take-home pharmacist pay. In October 2017, I transitioned our income from my salary job to my business. We live off my business income and use my salary for investments (like my business).

Not only that, but The Happy PharmD gained so much momentum. Our first biannual event, The Happy PharmD Summit, about transitioning into a new pharmacy career had over 2,500 attendees. I've grown classes that have now exceeded 400 pharmacist students.

First, I worked with trepidation, but that grew into acceptance and then jubilation. I found joy in letting go of the fear that had held me in my comfort zone, and now I find fulfillment every day helping fellow pharmacists achieve their goals and dreams.

Can you commit to doing the thing you know will make you happier?

So, What Comes Next?

You have a choice: make your career indispensable or opt for irrelevance. No one can predict the future, but I'd argue that no one should bank on the pharmacy landscape in 2020 looking the way it will in 2030. Innovation is as guaranteed as death and taxes. You cannot delay it (ask Firestone Tire & Rubber) or avoid it (ask Kodak). You can accept it with grace and evolve, or bury your head in the sand and face the eventual consequences: a worsening situation, increasing unhappiness, and a pink slip. It's uncomfortable to consider your job, *your livelihood*, in such stark terms. I know. I faced the same decision in my first real pharmacy role. After being forced into anticoagulation, I remember thinking, "There's no way I'll be doing anticoag forever. The newer medications will phase out warfarin. What I'm doing doesn't solve a long-term problem for the company." I recognized that it was just a matter of time until the price of drugs like Eliquis decreased and paying a pharmacist to provide warfarin management became more expensive. What if the cost of employing me exceeded the value I brought in? Well, I understood what that meant for my job security. The market always seeks to advance. I accepted that my job wouldn't be around forever, then I chose to innovate myself and developed skills outside pharmacy to make my career valuable—and I made myself much happier in the process.

So, what will you choose? Irrelevance or indispensability? Will you follow the path of your curiosity and unique ability, or stick with what drove you to pick up this book in the first place?

The choice is yours.

PROLOGUE

"Do you think you can help me?" asked Shama, a burned-out pharmacist at her wits end.

"Absolutely." I replied.

I've had the pleasure of working with extremely high-performing pharmacists, whose accolades you've probably seen online, and with pharmacists whose careers were in utter shambles. While I don't get to work with everyone who I come across, my earnest hope is that you read this book and implement at least one career strategy.

While I hope you take the advice from this book, I know the reality: implementing what you learn is difficult, especially when it's scary.

If you were encouraged, pushed, or driven by this book, I would be honored if you emailed me your story at *alex@thehappypharmd.com*.

I want to change this profession, and hear more stories like what happened to Shama. As I write these final words, I have a text message from her sitting in front of me: "Just got the offer."

Shama now works in a dream job. She's excited about work. She comes home happy again, enjoying the other parts of life that were meant to be filled with joy.

As I write this final section, I am teary eyed (just like when I cried at the multiple endings of *Lord of the Rings: Return of the King*). I think of all the other things I wish to include in this book. But if I don't finish this, then no one will ever read it!

My hope is to see you loving life because of your *Indispensable* career. Cheers.

BIOGRAPHY

Alex Barker, the founder of *The Happy PharmD*, helps pharmacists create fulfilling careers and lives. For a time, he was a burned-out clinical pharmacy specialist. Now, he's coached over 400 pharmacists to find new jobs, start businesses, and live their lives to the fullest. Alex loves experimenting with his life, such as doing a 30-day rejection challenge or reading one book every day for 66 days straight. All this experimenting made him a little odd, so he does things like paying off his house 27 years early.

When he's not working with pharmacists, he spends time with his wife, Megan, and two lovely girls, Izzie and Addie. He loves anime, family, reading, beet chips, pad Thai, Lord of the Rings, and Star Wars, but not in that order.

This book isn't for the pharmacists who love their jobs. Sure, the concepts, strategies, and lessons in these pages could make Indispensable an excellent supplement to their healthy careers—and I believe it will—but I didn't write it for them.